Crisis
of
Discipleship

Renewing the Art of Relational Disciple-making

Revised and Expanded Edition

By

G. Christopher Scruggs

Crisis of Discipleship:

Renewing the Art of Relational Disciple-making

Revised and expanded version

Not otherwise indicated scriptures are from the Holy Bible, English Standard Version. NIV. Copyright 1973, 1978, 1984. Scripture quotations noted "NIV," "NLT," or "Message," or other abbreviations indicated in the Bibliography are from the New International Version New Living Translation, the Message, or other noted translation or paraphrase. Such quotations are used with permission of the publisher and within their guidelines. Each publisher reserves all rights to their translation or paraphrase.

For information regarding permission to reprint material from this book, please mail your request to:

The Living Dialog Ministries
P.O. Box 15125
Richmond, VA 23227

Library of Congress in Publication Data:
G. Christopher Scruggs 1951-
Crisis of Discipleship: Renewing the Art of Relational Disciple-making
Includes bibliographical references

ISBN 979-8-9863804-5-2

Printed in the United States of America
Cover Design: Frank Gutbrod
Interior Design: Brian Regrut
Photo of Author:

I have had the pleasure of knowing and admiring Chris Scruggs from my arrival in Houston where it has been my privilege to serve the church where Chris returned to Christ through a Friday Night Bible Study, in 1977. During my time at FPC, I've had the pleasure of several conversations and email exchanges with Chris in which I came to understand and appreciate his deep passion for making disciples of Jesus Christ. His most recent book, *A Crisis Of Discipleship*, is a necessary challenge for a church that has had the "thinness" of our present state of discipleship exposed. I particularly resonated with his call for the church to recommit itself to becoming imitators of Christ in communities of love, worship and service. I found the book comprehensive, yet approachable and very practical. As one who has read many books on Christian discipleship, I would be happy to make this one of my primary recommendations.

> **Rev. Dr. James T. Birchfield**, former Senior Pastor,
> First Presbyterian Church, Houston, TX.

It is a great joy and high honor to recommend *Crisis of Discipleship*. I first met Chris Scruggs in seminary and he has been a personal friend and mentor for the last 30 years. The greatest resources on discipleship are developed within the church by people who love Christ and HIs bride. With the clarity of an experienced veteran, Chris has identified the challenges before the church. The principles he presents have been developed, field-tested and proven by a person who knows what it means to lead discipleship groups as both a lay leader and a pastor. As the church establishes its footing in a new decade, the framework presented here will fortify the Lord's people to fulfill the great commission with clarity, imagination and energy. This is a book we need.

> **The Reverend Dr. Bob Fuller**, Senior Pastor, First Presbyterian
> Church of San Antonio, Texas.

Having worked with Chris Scruggs for over ten years, as a co-pastor, I am very much aware of his strong intellect and his ability to apply such knowledge to the local church. Here Chris comes close to calling for a new reformation in Christ's Church. He also points the way to possible pathways to be taken in such a movement. A discipleship crisis can be healed if Chris's guidance is heeded.

> **Rev. Dr. Dave Schieber**, Pastor Emeritus of Advent Presbyterian
> Church in Cordova, Tennessee which he founded and where he
> served for over 30 years.

Rev. Chris Scruggs and I sat down over a Subway sandwich in September of 1994. I asked Chris, our newly installed pastor in Brownsville, Tennessee, what he wanted. He said we needed to start a men's group at the church that involved men from all walks of life from all over town. Chris left in 1999, but 28 years later, this group still meets weekly, and has grown to 40 men that fellowship, share a meal, have a devotional, raise money for needy causes, and pray on Thursdays at noon. After attending the Great Banquet in 1996, Rev. Chris Scruggs and seven other men that participated in this event, met each Sunday morning before Sunday School at the church to stay connected and be accountable to each other for the life-changing weekend we experienced in the three days at the Banquet. These 'reunion groups' helped each of us to keep our lives on track to serve God.

> **Dr. Robert Rooks. DDS**, Clerk of Session First Presbyterian Church of Brownsville, Tennessee on more than one occasion, but most specially in the year of 1994.

This book is an important call to the church and to all Christ-followers: Discipleship is essential and takes place best in intentional community. Chris provides a healthy examination of the current crisis and encourages us all to continue in the foundational work of making disciples who make disciples.

> **Sharon Brumagin**, Executive Director of Bay Presbyterian Church, Bay Village, Ohio and also former Young Life leader and parent.

The recent COVID health crisis has revealed many ways the church needs to grow, chief of which is reclaiming the primary call of Christ to make disciples of all nations. In *Crisis of Discipleship* Chris Scruggs not only diagnoses key hurdles to healthy discipleship but also (and more importantly) offers tools to empower discipleship. Chris makes discipleship invitational again, a need in our churches now more than any other time in our lifetime. Chris and Kathy make discipleship invitational with their lives and leadership, too, as they have led discipleship groups in our church and helped with training young adults in discipleship. This book is a treasure in a time of crisis of discipleship- A valuable resource for every Christian and Christian leader.

> **Mitchell Moore**, former missionary and Associate Pastor for Associate Pastor for Young Adults and Missions at First Presbyterian Church, San Antonio, Texas

I understand that the Chinese word for "crisis" can also be translated as "dangerous opportunity". Crisis is a time for reflecting in what has gone wrong in the past and speculating about what might happen in the future. It presents an opportunity to reassess priorities, to repent of past errors and to make new decisions. It reminds us also of how temporary many of our plans are, how subject we are to changes in the world around us and of how much we need to depend for our peace of mind on God's eternal changelessness. Your book very helpfully deals with two issues that are important in this crisis of discipleship. I hope that this book will have a wide readership for it merits careful study on both sides of the Atlantic – and beyond.

Rev. Ian Patterson, Minister Emeritus of St. Michael's Church, Linlithgow Scotland from 1977 until he retired. Before serving St. Michael's, he was chaplain of Stirling University and a missionary in Kenya. He was appointed one of Her Majesty's chaplains in 1997.

A great read for every believer and ministry leader! We must be about the hard work of building discipleship cultures centered on small groups that commit to authentic personal growth and Kingdom growth through multiplication. As Chris reminds us: Christ's call is simple but not easy: Go make disciples. Chris helps us all find our way back to the essential building blocks of disciple-making.

Libbie Peterson, retired head of small group ministry at Bay Presbyterian Church in Bay Village, Ohio.

This book by Chris Scruggs is a call to arms to Churches, pastors, Christian educators, and lay leaders to adopt a more appropriate strategy in this post-Christian era to make disciples that can mentor disciples and equip them to share the gospel of Jesus Christ with boldness and confidence. The format of the book offers practical ideas to overcome the discipleship crisis. It encourages believers to gather in small groups where they can learn together and be discipled via dialogue into a strong, vibrant faith communities. A wonderful journey of discovery awaits you. I strongly recommend this book for everyone who wants to confidently confront the 'Crisis of Discipleship" in America with the Word of Life, Jesus Christ.

John C. (Jack) Dannemiller, Chairman and CEO, Living Dialog Ministries, Richmond, VA

ACKNOWLEDGMENTS

My Christian walk began in Houston in the mid-1970s in a discipleship group called the "Friday Night Bible Study." Members of that group reflected God's wisdom and love, and my Christian walk began. For the next fourteen years, Kathy and I were part of small groups and Sunday School Classes in Houston. Each one made a difference in our lives.

In 1991, we went to Union Theological Seminary in Richmond, Virginia, where I was part of a small group ministry and attended Third Presbyterian Church. In 1994, we moved to Brownsville, Tennessee, where we continued to disciple people in a discipleship group format.

From 1999 until my "first" retirement, I was privileged to be co-pastor and then Senior Pastor of Advent Presbyterian Church, where we participated in many year-long small group Bible Studies and what we called "Reunion Groups" with a discipleship emphasis. We also encouraged missional small groups.

From 2017 until spring 2019, I was the Transitional Pastor and Staff Coach for Bay Presbyterian Church in Bay Village, Ohio. This church has a long heritage of small-group discipleship. It was in Bay Village that the initial draft of the book was written.

We have recently led a small discipleship group at First Presbyterian Church of San Antonio, Texas.

As always, the person who needs to be thanked most is my wife, Kathy. No one can write a book and be a fully engaged spouse simultaneously (or at least I can't). Kathy puts up with me, proofreads when asked, and gives endless suggestions whenever I write or lead a group. I could not count the bad decisions I might have made without her.

Many others have given support, inspiration, love, and correction; I am grateful to them. This book is dedicated to all the members of all the groups we have enjoyed over the years, particularly the Friday Night Bible Study, where it all began.

Crisis
of
Discipleship

Renewing the Art of Relational Disciple-making

TABLE OF CONTENTS

Preface

My wife, Kathy, and I have a life-long interest in discipleship. Before we were married, Kathy participated in young adult discipling programs. We met in a small Bible Study of young people who were Christians or seeking God. Over the last forty years, we have sponsored groups in our homes, businesses, schools, and churches. A few years ago, we published a practical workbook called *Salt & Light: Everyday Discipleship.* [1] *Salt & Light* explores one simple, helpful method for Christians and local congregations to make self-replicating disciples in an orderly and effective way. We continue to share our lives with others in mentoring relationships and discipleship groups.

The Crisis of Discipleship

My friend and fellow pastor, Dave Schieber, frequently says, "The Church is always one generation from extinction." [2] This is an important insight: the church in America is shrinking in numbers and influence. Christian faith no longer impacts the lives of many individuals and much of Western society. Even so-called "evangelical" groups, which multiplied during the post-World War II period, are shrinking. Many observers believe we are witnessing the Christian faith and practice collapse in America and the West.

Well-meaning denominations, churches, pastors, and others devise programs and strategies to stem the decline with mixed results. Many of them are good. Unfortunately, the problem cannot be addressed solely by strategy, programs, or advertising savvy. It can only be successfully addressed as individual Christians become fully committed disciples of Jesus, sharing God's wisdom and love with a broken world in obedience to the Great Commission. As a friend used to say, "We need to be totally sold out to God."

The Great Commission was not just given to twelve first-century people, professional clergy, and exceptionally gifted laypersons. Every Christian is intended to share the Good News and help mature disciples who respond to God's call. *Crisis of Discipleship* clarifies some of the causes of the problem of disciple-mak-

1

ing in our culture and suggests a possible strategy to respond. Hopefully, readers will be empowered to understand the crisis of discipleship more profoundly and effectively, share their Christian faith with others, and lead other church members in the way of Christ.

The Danger of Cheap Grace

In the 1930s, the German theologian, Dietrich Bonhoeffer, wrote a Christian classic, *The Cost of Discipleship*, in which he spoke about the danger of "Cheap Grace." [3] Today, perhaps because institutional churches in the West did not take the implications of *The Cost of Discipleship* seriously, Christians face a "crisis of discipleship," which is the theme of this book.

As a friend recently said, "We have lost an entire generation for the Church and are in danger of losing another." Christians can respond to the challenge to reach the next and lost generations with the Good News of the wisdom and love of God. However, we cannot overcome our discipleship crisis until and unless individual Christians and congregations are motivated to be more authentic disciples of Christ. For this to happen, Christians must take seriously the Great Commandment, the Great Commission, and the importance of discipling new believers.

When beginning a long journey, it is best to look at a map, especially the difficult roads we may have to travel. *Crisis of Discipleship* begins with an analysis of the emerging postmodern world—a culture rapidly becoming worldwide due to the globalization of Western culture over the past 300 years, particularly of American culture in the second half of the 20th Century. This is the most challenging section of the book, but it is critical to move forward wisely.

Having set the stage by analyzing the problem, *Crisis of Discipleship* shares one historical, Biblical understanding of how Christians can share their faith in the face of these challenges. It addresses the contemporary implications of the Great Commission to "Go everywhere and make disciples of everyone you can, bringing them to faith and teaching these new disciples to follow the teachings of the Messiah, who will always be present with those who go about the business of making disciples" (Matthew 28:16-21, paraphrase).

The book is designed for readers who wish to learn more about the Way of Jesus and how to share that way with others. I am not a scholar, and the book is not a theological treatise. It is a mixture of practical discipleship theory and practice designed to help leaders and others understand barriers our culture places in the path of those who desire to share the Way of Christ in a relationship of wisdom and love with others. On the other hand, *Crisis of Discipleship* is not a "how-to book." There are many such books, some of them quite good. Instead, this book looks at the underlying causes of our difficulties and the best general strategy to respond. Each reader and each congregation must choose its particular way of responding to the crisis of discipleship we face.

Two basic ideas unify the essays:

First, God is Love and exists in a loving family-like relationship, Father, Son, and Holy Spirit. Therefore, the Christian faith is best shared in loving communal interaction. This excludes all ideas of force, physical, mental, emotional, and otherwise. No one comes to authentic faith other than freely.

Second, God is Light, and the Christian faith should be shared with the patience, wisdom, and restraint characteristic of our wise and patient God. The light of Christ speaks for itself and does not need pressure tactics or advertising savvy to succeed.

If Christians keep these two ideas in mind, many mistakes in evangelism and discipleship can be avoided.

May the Lord bless and keep each and every reader of this book.

Chris Scruggs
Pentecost 2023

PART 1:

COME AND FOLLOW ME

CHAPTER 1

The Blessed Life

We live in a curious age. Never in human history have people in the developed world had so much material wealth. Paradoxically, never have people experienced more anxiety about the future, their ability to continue to consume at or above their current level, and especially the meaning and purpose of their lives. Young people in almost all Western democracies, most notably in the United States, the so-called "leader of the free world," are often characterized by a lack of interest in the way of life and faith in the institutions that provide them with the highest standard of living and the most personal freedom experienced anywhere in human history.

Sadly, among Christians, fewer and fewer people live as fully committed disciples. Europe's churches are nearly empty, and those in the United States and North America are rapidly going down the same path. People have lost trust in that way of life that made our civilization possible.

Social commentators, Christian and non-Christian, liberal and conservative, traditionalist and radical, agree that something is wrong. They don't agree on what is wrong, how serious the problem is, or what to do in response, but they agree there is a problem. Often, articles are published with titles like "Are America's best days behind her?"[1] These articles focus on indications that something is deeply wrong with our culture.

Frequently, commentators conclude that the root of our society's problems is that material wealth, prosperity, pleasure, consumption, leisure, and the like cannot provide meaning, purpose, love, or inner strength and security. The relentless search for meaning and purpose by the means advocated by our society results in a loss of meaning, purpose, love, inner strength, and security. The result is pervasive loneliness, isolation, neurosis, and anxiety.

One reason we have so much trouble resisting the temptations of our culture is that most people have a deeply ingrained, culturally-formed notion of "the Good Life." The good life involves feelings of personal pleasure and happiness. Most people believe that hard work, education, healthy habits, exercise, pleasurable experiences, travel, recreation, hobbies, and other forms of "self-actualization" are essential to experiencing personal fulfillment. Some believe government can and should create this good life for its citizens. Others think it should be formed by private industry and individual initiative. However, people consciously and subconsciously hope for an earthly paradise in which all human expectations and desires are met.[2]

Jesus and the Blessed Life

Jesus never talked about the desirability of living to old age, attaining physical beauty, staying fit and healthy, acquiring wealth, getting ahead financially, consuming increasing amounts of goods and services, traveling, having pleasurable experiences, or any of the central preoccupations of our day. However, he did speak about what he called "the blessed life."

Interestingly, Jesus' teachings concerning the blessed life contradict our culture's idea of the blessed life. Today, when people use the word "blessed," it usually involves something concrete we have received. We say, "I am blessed with good health." "I am blessed with a strong heart." "I am blessed with a wonderful spouse." "I am blessed with healthy children." "I am blessed financially." "I am blessed with a new job." "I am blessed with a promotion." The list of such blessings goes on and on, but they have this in common: they relate to physical benefits that contribute to our emotional and physical well-being.

On the other hand, in the Sermon on the Mount, Jesus says things like,

> Blessed are the poor in spirit.
> Blessed are those who mourn.
> Blessed are the humble.
> Blessed are the merciful.
> Blessed are the pure in heart.
> Blessed are the peacemakers.

Worst of all, Jesus says,

> Blessed are the persecuted. [3]

In Luke, Jesus' words are even less palatable to modern ears.[4]   In Luke, Jesus is recorded saying, "Blessed are the poor," not just the poor in spirit. He says, "Blessed are the hungry," not just those who hunger and thirst for righteousness. He says, "Blessed are those who weep," and repeats, "Blessed are you when men hate you, exclude you, and insult you." [5]   Jesus seems to be saying that everything contemporary society believes characterizes the blessed life does not and what the modern world considers contrary to the blessed life is a trustworthy source of blessing.

Jesus challenges our human presuppositions about what it means to be blessed. For Jesus, the blessed life is not something **exterior** to ourselves that we acquire, like money, power, pleasure, and the like. Instead, blessedness flows from **internal** qualities we develop. Moreover, because of its very nature, the blessed life is not something we naturally seek but must instead desire as a gift. The exterior life, upon which modern people place so much emphasis, is secondary. It is our relationship with God and with his plans and purposes that are primary. In other words, by the wisdom of Jesus, our society has things entirely backward!

Our natural way of looking at the world prevents us from seeing and understanding the blessed life without God's intervention. [6]   The blessed life is received by faith in God and his Word. We cannot discover by ourselves. To receive this blessing, someone inspired by the Spirit must tell us about the blessed life and show us what it looks like. We need help to overcome our cultural addictions to power, pleasure, and possessions. That is why Christ came. In the end, God, by the power of the Holy Spirit, must work inside us so that we can receive by faith what God has promised.

The Old Testament and the Blessed Life

The Old Testament reflects an understanding that the blessed life, like all of life, is a gift from God. The Hebrew word "Baruch" implies a kind of all-completeness and sense of wholeness and well-being that can only come from God. God creates the human race in the creation story and immediately blesses them (Gen. 1:27-28). God's blessing to Adam and Eve implies that the human race was intended to occupy and enjoy God's creation as creatures that joyfully appreciate and participate in the completion of God's intention for that creation.

The story of the fall reflects the human propensity to turn away from our divine destiny of blessing (Gen. 3:16-19). The curse of the fall described in Genesis is not the abusive action of an angry God. It is the inevitable result of leaving the path of fellowship with God for self-centeredness and self-seeking—a decision that always leads to alienation, misguided behavior, and suffering. The human race, meant for communion with God, nature, and one another, forfeits its divine destiny and restlessly roams the earth in search of a restoration of blessing.

In Noah's story, God saves a righteous man amid a catastrophe of sin and alienation that engulfs the world. When the flood is over, Noah departs from the ark, builds an altar, and praises God. God, in return, blesses Noah in language that reveals His desire to restore the blessing lost in the garden of Eden: "Then God blessed Noah and his children saying to them, 'Be fruitful and multiply'" (Gen. 9:1).[7] Even in judgment, God is restoring, renewing, and blessing the human race.

Abraham's story reaches a decisive moment when God calls him into a new and unique blessing relationship. When the Lord calls him to leave his country, his people, and those of his household left behind, he promises:

> I will make you into a great nation,
>   and I will bless you;
> I will make your name great,
>   and you will be a blessing.
> I will bless those who bless you,
>   and whoever curses you I will curse;
>   and all peoples on earth will be blessed through you.
>   (Genesis 12:2-3)

The blessing God gives to Abraham is not just for his genetic family. It is a blessing for the entire world and every tribe and nation. It is a blessing for everyone on earth. This blessing flows from the intimate, trustful relationship Abraham and his family are intended to have with God. As the story unfolds, it is evident that the blessing extends from Abraham and his family to the entire world (See Gen. 18:18; 22:18; 28:14). The blessing through the faith Abraham demonstrated continues today.

Blessings and the Wise Life

The book of Psalms begins by describing the blessed life and how to achieve it. The great hymnbook of the Bible begins as follows:

> Blessed are those who do not walk in the counsel of godlessness,
> nor stand in the path of sinners, nor sit in the seat of scoffers;
> But delight in the teachings of the One Who Was, Is, and Will Be,
> day and night meditating on the Way of the LORD.
>
> Followers of this Way are like trees planted by streams of water,
> sending down deep roots, producing the fruit of a good life.
> Such people do not shrivel up in heated or difficult times

what they undertake in wisdom and love brings new life.

(Psalm 1:1-3, author's paraphrase)

By the time this psalm was written, the people of Israel understood that the blessed life is achieved by following God's teachings. The psalmists believed God reveals in nature and his word a way of life that leads to blessing. The blessed person receives the gift of fellowship with God and the physical benefits that accompany obedience to God's instructions. Those who follow the way of wickedness (act contrary to God's will) can never be blessed. They have chosen a path that leads away from blessing.

Wisdom literature affirms the same idea: the blessed life is lived according to the wisdom God embedded in the universe, which is revealed for the people of God in God's teachings contained in the scriptures (Proverbs 3:13-18). [8] Those who follow the path of wisdom (adapting their lives to divine and created reality) find a path leading to peace and plenty. Blessings are received by those who develop a wisdom God embedded in the universe. The Path of Life is the Path of Wisdom, the most valuable gift a person can receive and the ground and source of all the blessings of life. [9]

The blessed life is achieved by wisdom that comes only from God and fellowship with God. The blessed person listens to the voice of God's wisdom and waits for God's revelation of the proper course of action in the practical affairs of life (Proverbs 8:34). Ultimately, the intelligent life is a life of wise, loving, trustful, and faithful conformity to God's character and will (Proverbs 16:20). It cannot be achieved without the deep reverence and respect for God that that Bible terms, "the fear of the Lord," which is the beginning of wisdom and the blessed life (Proverbs 1:6, 9:10; 28:14). [10]

Blessing and the Prophetic Life

If wisdom literature emphasizes that the blessed life results from gaining wisdom, the Prophets teach that the blessed life results from following God's will and obeying his teachings in practical and political affairs. The prophets interpreted Israel's failure to retain its freedom and independence, defeat by the Assyrians and Babylonians, and exile to Babylon as a judgment on Israel's lack of faithfulness to the God of Abraham. As a result of this failure, God removed his blessing and allowed judgment to come upon Israel. The people of God forfeited the blessed life.

If the recipe of the wisdom writers for blessing was to forsake foolishness and wickedness and seek the "Path of Life," the prophets recommended that Israel return to faith in the Living God and live according to God's instructions and will.[11]   Their message was one of religious and national revival. "In returning and rest you shall be saved; in quietness and in trust shall be your strength" (see Isaiah 30:15; Jeremiah 3:22, 4:1). If Israel returned to faithfulness to God, they would be restored to their land, and the blessings of God would return. [12]

Old Testament writers were aware of the role chance, good fortune, and bad luck play in human life. [13]   Nevertheless, they believed God was the source of the good life and all the blessings of life, physical, emotional, mental, and spiritual. Even in the early stages of its development, the idea of a restored Kingdom of David was more than a restored earthly kingdom, but a kingdom of wisdom, righteousness, and peace. As the Old Testament closes, the people of God await the coming of the promised Messiah who will rescue and deliver them.

The New Testament and the Blessed Life

By Jesus' time, the religion of Israel had developed in a disturbing way. Liturgically, the blessed life was achieved by participating in religious rituals and making proper sacrifices. In terms of behavior, the blessed life was achieved through understanding the law of Moses and following its details as interpreted by the rabbis. The Pharisees and teachers of the law developed a detailed understanding of what it meant to follow the law in every area of life. For the religious few, this form of life gave meaning and purpose. For the average person, temple religion had become a matter of mere external expression, and the faith of the scribes and Pharisees was a complicated and unachievable set of rules.

When Jesus walked beside the Sea of Galilee and called twelve ordinary people to become his followers, he revealed something exciting: The blessed life is not achieved by external religious observances, the devoted study of the law, or detained observance of rules. Instead, discipleship and the blessed life are a matter of a living relationship with a personal God, the source of wisdom and love. Jesus called his disciples into a personal relationship, and through that relationship, into a personal relationship with God so they might see the knowledge and love he embodied daily. As with any relationship, the defining characteristic of Jesus' way was a personal commitment to love we call "faith." The faith of the original disciples was reflected by their decision to trust and follow Jesus.

It took the disciples a long time to understand that the blessed life Jesus promised was not a promise of uninterrupted affluence, health, success, pleasure, or victory over opposition. The crucified Messiah revealed a blessing that transcends human wisdom and human capacity to achieve (I Cor. 1:16ff), which is why Jesus says, "Peace I leave with you; my peace I give you. I do not give to you as the world gives. Do not let your hearts be troubled and do not be afraid" (John 14:27).

The Truly Blessed Life

So then, what is a blessed life? The blessed life is lived in fellowship with God, nature, and others. It is lived in solidarity with the external world as human beings recover the stewardship of creation for which the human race was created. It is a life of restored interpersonal relationships, as the alienation caused by pride, selfishness, and self-seeking is overcome. The blessed life is a life of spiritual and emotional wholeness. It is a life of restored communion with God.

The person who lives in communion with God, creation, and other human beings achieves emotional and spiritual wholeness. The blessed life is a life of humility and acceptance of others because the wise person recognizes that human beings are fallible, finite, and capable of wickedness. The blessed life is a life of steadfast love because those who live in a relationship with God exhibit that unshakable love in their day-to-day lives.

Certain forms of modern Christianity resemble the religion of Israel at the end of the Old Testament. People continue to attend church; some study the Bible and attempt to organize their lives "according to biblical principles." Sometimes, their understanding of these principles is detailed and complex. However, for most people, the life of discipleship lived under grace has become a dim memory. Just as with the ancient Israelites, for many people today, the life of faith seems complicated, unrewarding, and unachievable. [14]

When I was a young Christian, the missionary, evangelist, and social theologian Francis Schaeffer diagnosed the condition of Western society as dominated by a definition of the good life as achieving personal peace and affluence. [15] Indeed, our society is dominated by the individualistic search for things, experiences, recreation, and a sense of happiness and peace. However, amid this search, we experience a high level of dysfunction.

Why is this so? Is it because the "Blessed Life" cannot be found in having more things, achieving success, experiencing pleasures, and the like? What if the blessed life can only be found in the humble search for wisdom in daily living and loving service to God and others? What if our society and every other society have always been misguided at a deep level concerning what constitutes a blessed life? [16]

If people in contemporary society could achieve a blessed life by reading about it, our society would already be blessed. There are many, many self-help books. There are books about how to lose weight, gain weight, exercise, take vitamins, think and grow rich, retire early, become more physically able to defend ourselves, and find peace with God or the Ultimate (however you visualize it). There are books about anything and everything we might do to achieve a blessed life on our own terms. My experience, and the experience of most people who've tried these strategies, is that they don't permanently work.

Human beings need more than information to achieve a blessed life. We need to experience a blessed life. We need to experience what it is to live wisely. We need to experience what it is like to have healthy relationships with other people. We need to experience what it is like to love others with what the Bible calls "steadfast love" or "agape love," God's self-giving, long-suffering, faithful love. For people to experience the blessed life, there must be disciples who follow Jesus and don't just read books. [17] People must experience the blessed life in a community formed by the wisdom and love of God in Christ.

Like today, the disciples did not immediately understand or emulate what Jesus showed them. Like us, they did not learn all at once but needed a long period of observation and personal interaction. It was not until after his death and resurrection that they understood. Although Peter was inspired to say that Jesus was the Christ, the Son of the living God, at Caesarea Philippi, his inspiration was temporary. He would still deny Jesus and go back to fishing until his time of training and preparation was complete. Only after he saw the risen Christ and experienced the power of the resurrection did Peter become capable of living the blessed life. [18]

We cannot expect people in our time to be any different. Transformational understanding comes slowly. It requires time, practice, mistakes, correction, teaching, patience, and all the other attributes of discipleship. Jesus created and lived in a relationship with his disciples during his earthly ministry because relationships are the only way people can truly be transformed. In our day and time, we are experiencing a crisis of discipleship precisely because we have not done a particularly good job of discipling others into a living relationship with God. The discipleship crisis will only abate once we give up the idea that better marketing, worship, or programming can achieve real change. Real change is found in recovering Jesus' understanding of the Blessed Life and the way of life Jesus offers.

Christians who minister within the European and North American context have a unique opportunity. Our mission is to take people where we find them, caught in damaging cultural patterns, and wisely and lovingly shepherd them into the way of Christ. The challenge posed by Western culture involves the need to minister with an understanding that the way of Christ and the way of this world are radically different. The need is to develop the kind of character that builds and sustains the Christian community in the face of enormous cultural challenges.

Merely repeating past truisms in past ways will not work. Faith divorced from a distinctive, communal way of life will not work. Cheap grace is dispensed for sins few people either acknowledge as sins or believe are sins will not work. Only the truth embodied in love will do. Until Christians adapt to the challenges of our society, we will be trapped in a crisis of discipleship.

— CHAPTER 2 —

Life in the Ruins

Why is it so difficult to communicate the Christian faith in contemporary society? Why is our culture so resistant to the gospel message of God's love for the human race? How can we Christians improve our ability to share the Gospel? These are essential questions. The first step to being an effective witness is understanding those we seek to reach. If we want to strengthen our witness to our culture, Christians need to understand better the culture and the barriers to faith that result from how contemporary people see the world.

The Challenge of Discipleship in Our Culture

Christians proclaim Jesus is "The Way, The Truth, and the Life." For those who believe that declaration is essential and life-changing. For most non-Christians, the words are meaningless. In their way of thinking, people choose a lifestyle that pleases them. They do not believe there is a God-given "way," "truth," or "life." There are only personal perspectives of people. There is no inherent goodness or beauty. There is one kind of life, what the ancient Greeks called "Bios,"—the bodily life of the human-animal. There is no moral or spiritual life not reducible to biology. Jesus is not "the Way, the Truth, and the Life" because no moral and spiritual "Way, Truth, and Life" exists or can exist.

The decline of Christian faith parallels the ascendancy of a secular modern world and the gradual emergence of what scholars call "a post-Christian era."[1] Christians have been slow to see and respond to the dramatic shift in our culture—a culture Christianity helped create and sustain, which Christians generally assume should be receptive to their religious vision. As a retired professor observed, "We were slow to discern that the culture is no longer our friend."[2] The church has been slow to recognize that a new dominant worldview has replaced a Christian worldview as the primary way people structure reality in Western society.

This new worldview has been artfully summarized in the following way:

> We are alone in the physical universe, which constitutes the only
> reality. This universe has no embedded notion of truth, beauty, or
> goodness. These concepts are matters of personal choice. Humans
> must, therefore, create their own meaning and lives by acts of per-
> sonal preference. All attempts to force such ideas upon others is
> a form of coercion by which one group forces its will upon others.
> Personal pleasure attained by the acquisition of personal expe-
> riences and things that can provide desired experiences are how
> humans create their lives. [3]

Sociologists remind us that all people live in cultures characterized by "plausibility structures" that define what is reasonable and what is not. The secular
plausibility structure of modern society creates an automatic "crisis of credibil-
ity" within which Christian beliefs, values, and morals no longer make sense to
many people, especially the youngest, best-educated, and most successful members of the cultural elite. [4]

A World of "Rocks and Forces"

A profoundly materialistic worldview sits beneath our culture's hostility to
religious faith and its increasing inability to understand or appreciate faith. People in Western culture intuitively assume that the material world is fundamental and that science and technology are the best ways to explore and relate to
the real world. Deep in the contemporary psyche is the notion that the physical
universe is the only and ultimate reality. In this view, all that "really" exists are
material things and forces that act upon them. [5] This results in a perception that
human beings are isolated individuals, cut off from others and bound to others
only by personal, emotional, psychic, or material forces. [6]

Among churches, there are increasingly desperate attempts to survive within
this worldview. [7] In "liberal" circles, this is evident in its theological accommodation to the materialistic and anti-supernatural worldview of modernity.
In "evangelical" circles, the accommodation takes a different form, such as an
uncritical adoption of psychotherapeutic techniques and entertainment-focused
worship. In conservative churches, there is often a wholesale philosophical rejection of modernity, coupled with an uncritical acceptance of its means, methods, and goals. [8] In both cases, genuinely life-changing discipleship is nearly
impossible.

What is needed is a way forward in which modernity's intellectual and practical achievements are recognized and appreciated, but its limitations and failures

are also understood and pointed out. "Liberal" Christianity makes an error when it reduces Christian faith to the categories of modernity, and "conservative" Christianity makes an equally foolish mistake when it fails to accept, understand, and celebrate the accomplishments of the modern world.

Contemporary scientific understanding of the world does not support the materialistic worldview that emerged in the 18th and 19th centuries. It is vital that Christians not reject technology or science but instead understand and embrace the vision of reality that science discerns concerning the universe in which we live. [9] The emerging scientific view of reality, in many ways, supports a Christian view of reality in which there is acceptance of non-material reality and the potential for God, ideal truths, such as Truth, Goodness, and Beauty—and for a "Way, Truth, and Life" in communion with God and the world, both seen and unseen, aesthetic, conceptual, ethical, material, and moral. [10]

Features of Contemporary Culture

There are features of the recent, late modern worldview that profoundly impact discipleship and disciple-making and make our culture intuitively hostile to the gospel's message. Here are a few of the most important:

"Truth is Whatever is True for Me"

Nothing is more common than to hear people voice the opinion that "all truth is relative." [11] In our culture, when applied to faith and morals, "true" means "true for me," as opposed to "true" in the sense of accurately rendering an external reality independent of my ideas about it. Beauty means "beautiful to me." "Good" means "seems good to me." A popular way of expressing this aspect of postmodernity is, "You have your truth; I have mine." In a society characterized by this kind of thinking, it is difficult to make persuasive, unpopular, or counter-cultural truth claims, especially religious claims, such as the claim that "Jesus is Lord." Such claims are dismissed as silly or prejudiced.

In our culture, truth claims are increasingly seen as nothing more than an attempt by the person making a claim to gain advantage, control, or power over another person or group. While it is positive to understand that all expressions of truth inevitably involve the social condition and bias of the claimant, this feature is often overwhelmed by an adverse inference that there is no objective moral or other reality outside of isolated individuals, who ought to be able to live, think, and act as they see fit. It is essential to understand that while people make claims intended to gain some degree of control over another person or institution, not all truth claims or moral claims are motivated by the desire for power over another person. Some truth claims are motivated by a conviction that the person making such a claim has discerned an important aspect of reality and wishes to share that discovery with another person whom it may help.

Christianity has a robust response to the nihilistic vision of radical postmodern thinking. The foundation of what is sometimes called "the postmodern worldview" lies in the idea that all truth claims involve bids for power. Thus, a claim that Jesus Christ is the Son of God is seen as nothing but a claim for control over people's lives. Christian faith is, however, essentially exempt from this interpretation. The fundamental insight of Christian faith is that God is a person (not an idea) characterized by self-giving, self-sacrificing love (not power-seeking) (1 John 4:8).

In Christ, God forsook all power and privilege for the sake of the human race and gave God's-self for the world in a supreme act of sacrificial love. (Philippians 2:5-11). Far from being a bid for power, the Christian faith accepts God's self-giving sacrificial love. This love is given to the beloved in the hope of a free response of love from the other. No one coming to faith is forced or coerced by God, for that would violate the love with which the offer of a relationship is made. While Christians often not do not live up to this ideal, the Biblical story speaks of God forsaking power in love for the world's sake.

"I Alone Get to Make all my Choices"

Contemporary society is hostile to tradition, authority, and historic communal norms that might impact an individual's "free choice." [12] Modern people instinctively question authority and historical social norms. The bias of the modern age against authority and tradition is reflected in the radical selfishness that permeates Western culture. The good life involves my ability to do "whatever I want so long as I do not hurt anyone else." [13] In such a culture, the idea that individual desires and goals may need to be sacrificed for the good of parents, children, city, state, or nation seems quaint and out of date.

In recent years, radical individualism has moved from being the province of an intellectual and cultural elite to being an underlying assumption of the vast majority of people. For most people today, traditional sources of authority, such as parents, pastors, religious communities, business and political leaders, and the authority of such intellectual works, like the Bible, are either lost or significantly undermined. The result is increasing personal and social dysfunction. [14]

"If it Feels Good, I Should Do It."

Without question, the dominant moral philosophy of early twenty-first-century America is hedonism. [15]   The idea that the good life is synonymous with a life of personal pleasure is part of the everyday environment within which most people live. Hedonism surrounds and permeates our culture. The idea that pleasure, especially physical pleasure, is the ultimate good bombards people daily from television, movies, media, and music in an endless barrage of moral relativism.

A subtle form of this hedonism is often found among Christians. Many Christians who would never overtly affirm their commitment to a life lived solely for pleasure engage in activities indistinguishable from non-Christians' activities. Often, Christians have affairs, drink heavily, use recreational drugs, collect pleasurable experiences, are financially greedy, and engage in other hedonistic activities no less frequently than non-Christians. Despite what Christians, including church leaders, may say about the meaning of religious faith, a silent internal, secular worldview impacts everything from the family budget to the cars they drive, to the time spent on hobbies, to personal fitness and grooming, to their genuine commitment to other people. [16]

"What is Right is What is Right for Me"

Our culture's radical individualism and moral hedonism combine with the modern awareness of cultural differences in fundamental belief systems to create the moral and spiritual relativism that characterizes many people's moral and religious beliefs and behavior. [17]   Often, people do not so much reject traditional moral standards as they disregard their application to themselves or other persons who do not see them as personally "right for them." This way of thinking puts Christian leaders, whose teaching and preaching involves moral issues, in a dilemma: Christians must either speak in unpopular ways and live with the resulting rejection or silently appear to conform the teachings of the Scriptures and Church to contemporary moral norms. Many choose the latter course.

During one of my advanced degree programs, I saw the essential irrationality of this modern way of thinking demonstrated in a student conversation. During a class, the notion of radical moral relativism was advanced. After class, a group continued the discussion. Finally, one participant asked one proponent of the moral relativistic position, "Do you mean that there is no moral difference between a tribe of pigmies that engage in human sacrifice and Christian morals?" Before the person thought, he answered, "Yes." The group went quiet as people confronted the implications of what they had been taught in their undergraduate and graduate programs.

"I Alone Am Responsible for My Life Story"

Scholars tell us that human beings are, by nature, narrative thinkers. [18] We instinctively place our lives within the context of a story in which we are the main character. In previous societies, there was a kind of over-arching story, what scholars call a "meta-narrative," that allowed people to live into a personal story in which their life made sense and had meaning and purpose. Old Testament stories of Abraham, Isaac, Jacob, Esau, and the patriarchs, Moses, Deborah, Joshua, and the exilic generation; Gideon and the Judges, Saul, David, Abigail, Bathsheba, and Solomon; and the decline of David's kingdom and its fall provided for ancient Israel a meaningful story around which human life could be structured. [19] The story of Jesus and his life, death, and resurrection functioned this way for much of Europe and North and South America.

A particular challenge for contemporary Christians in sharing the Christian story is that we live in a "world that has lost its story." [20] Our culture is characterized by rejecting any overarching story that seeks to give meaning and direction to human life. Not only do contemporary people not believe the Christian story, they often do not believe there is any meaningful story around which to order their lives. The result is a kind of endless series of life experiences and decisions based not upon a vision of the future but upon momentary and passing notions of what might be fun or life-enhancing. In the process, many people end up physically, morally, spiritually, and emotionally injured.

Christians have traditionally believed that the story of God's relationship with humanity as rendered in the Jewish and Christian Bible (the Old and New Testaments), and especially in the story of the life, death, and resurrect of Jesus and the writings of the New Testament authors provided a story-line into which their individual lives found meaning and purpose. It is precisely this kind of meta-narrative postmodern thinking rejects. [21]

"The One Who Dies with the Most Toys Wins"

When people from less developed nations visit Europe and North America, they immediately notice the vast array of goods and services available to those living in these cultures. (Often, they bring a list of items to purchase for friends and loved ones that are difficult or expensive to acquire back home.) America and Europe have become giant shopping centers.

A culture without an overarching meaning and purpose will likely find consumerism attractive and distracting. With the passing of the World War II generation, most Americans cannot remember a time not characterized by relative prosperity. The standard of living most Americans enjoy surpasses that of their grandparents and great-grandparents. The impact of consumerism on the culture is profound and pervasive.

The economies of Europe and North America have evolved from struggling to meet basic human needs to providing an ever-growing supply of goods and services to an affluent consumer market. Marketing has moved from a means by which people with basic needs find products to meet those needs to the creation of needs in ever-increasing, narrow product niches. The definition of the "good life" is dominated by the feeling that "good" and "abundant" are identical concepts.

A consumer culture challenges the gospel, the Church, and its leaders. Many members of local congregations have difficulty resisting consumerism; however, church leaders and their families are not exempt from the disease called "consumeritis." [22]   Consumerism assumes that human happiness can be purchased, that the acquisition of things will bring happiness, and that the experience of ownership and possession is redemptive. Few people explicitly articulate this faith, but many people practice it. The bumper sticker that reads, "He who dies with the most toys wins," is truer for more people than they want to admit, including many who would never admit that things constitute the primary focus of their lives.

The False Gospel of "Entertainment"

Into the emptiness created by the loss of a meaningful story to guide our society, the entertainment industry provides endless hedonistic and increasingly nihilistic narratives to replace the Biblical story. Media and entertainment are central to the lives of modern people. Unfortunately, the vision shared is often shallow, simplistic, adolescently romantic, obsessed with sex, and violent. The communication techniques make consciously irrational emotional appeals, resulting in a culture saturated with the values of the entertainment media. One author describes it in the following manner:

> For all practical purposes, the U.S. today is a 24-hour TV entertainment society. Everything in contemporary America is entertainment, from sporting events to big business, politics, certainly religion, and even academia. If it isn't fun, cute, or packaged in a

ten-second sound bite, then forget it. If it can't be presented with a smiling, cheerful, sexy face, then it ain't worth it. We're all spectators in a grand entertainment society. [23]

Recently, my wife and I watched a television show that exemplifies the problems with the contemporary entertainment industry. The show's storyline concerns young people who can travel backward in time. [24] Two different groups are attempting to influence the direction of human history. Roughly speaking, one group is portrayed as "bad guys" and the other as "good guys." The good guys kill just as many people and act irrationally as the bad guys, except they are trying to "protect human freedom." The bad guys are trying to control the future for their political and economic interests. The bad guys are mere caricatures of the people the media industry dislikes.

The show is saturated by human self-assertion and ethical chaos. The characters struggle with the idea that there might be a higher power who controls the future, but of course, there isn't one active in their plotline, so they must struggle to create a meaningful future all on their own. They have to make choices.

Deep in the moral incoherency of the show is what Walter Wink calls "the myth of redemptive violence" – the notion that violence can be redemptive if only the "good guys" defeat the "bad guys." (It's not redemptive for bad guys to kill good guys.) [25] The result is a constant replay of a shallow, relativistic philosophy the writers were probably taught in High School and College. In addition, because the show takes the watcher back into history, occasionally, the watcher is treated to a shallow, cartoon version of world history, sometimes distorted.

A society dominated by entertainment reduces complex problems to sound bites and catchy lyrics. Gone are the human race's fundamental moral and spiritual dilemmas, which are replaced by a simplistic one-hour drama. A media-saturated society allows people to view sex and violence without consequences. News depictions of our politics have become similarly shallow. If politicians often oversimplify complex problems, the media has largely lost interest in educating the public on the facts, which are often complex and challenging to understand, finding it easier to give opinion pieces and distorted coverage of current events. Complicated problems cannot receive proper attention. They are too complex, and solutions would require self-denial in a culture addicted to self and selfish consumption.

This culture of oversimplification impacts discipleship because of the pressure to communicate the Christian faith, Scripture, Christian theology, and the principles of Christian life in simple, even simplistic, ways. Furthermore, how worship services and other church programs are conceived and presented are increasingly shaped by how the entertainment industry structures reality and the acquisition of new information and ideas. None of this is necessarily helpful in communicating the historic Christian faith.

The Dysfunctional Result

Our culture cannot sustain and renew its intellectual, moral, political, economic, and spiritual foundations because of its fundamental assumptions about reality and life. The result is increasing social descent into radical individualism and moral and spiritual relativism. [26] We see evidence of this in every aspect of our society. There is good news: In fundamental ways, the cultural ruins around us indicate that the Christian story is more fruitful and life-enhancing than the secular story that increasingly replaces it.

Our "Postmodern," Neo-Pagan Context

Our culture is often referred to as "postmodern." I believe the term "postmodern" is deceiving and not always helpful. [27] All postmodern connotes is that we live "after" the modern era. Many characteristics of what is commonly called "postmodern" may indicate only the nihilistic end-phase of the modern era. [28] Whatever the case, we are entering a new period of human history, but it is unclear what the future will be like. Just as with the end of the Greco-Roman and Medieval eras, the result is confusion and social dislocation.

In some ways, the culture we inhabit involves a return to paganism. Unlike the ancient world, with its gods and goddesses embodying natural powers, our cultural paganism is a "religionless paganism." [29] In such a culture, discipleship must be lived out without the social support common in preceding generations. America, in particular, has shifted from one in which Protestantism, especially mainline Protestantism, represents a societal religious and moral consensus to a society where many cultural elites are often openly hostile to Christian faith and morals. [30]

The Challenge to Discipleship

A culture characterized by consumerism, radical individualism, hedonism, moral relativism, religious pluralism, materialism, "consumeritus," and "entertainmentism" is a challenging culture in which to proclaim the gospel and form a Christian community. It is common in conversations, particularly with older pastors, where the following statement is made. "It is no longer fun to be in ministry." The "burnout" level among pastors and religious leaders is increasing, so many are leaving the ministry.

In noting the reactions of Third World observers to American cultural religion, Eugene Peterson makes an observation that, at least partially explains this sentiment:

> What they notice mostly is greed, silliness, and narcissism. They
> appreciate the size and prosperity of our churches, the energy, and
> the technology. Still, they wonder at the conspicuous absence of
> the cross, the phobic avoidance of suffering, the puzzling indiffer-
> ence to community, and relationships of intimacy. [31]

The culture of early twenty-first-century Europe and America is deeply at odds with the gospel and a form of life based on the Christian narrative. The dominant cultural patterns constitute a form of life at odds with values at the core of the Christian faith and the kind of life the gospel narrative encourages Christians to lead. Unsurprisingly, the church and Christians struggle to adapt and respond to this emerging reality.

As hostility toward the Christian faith has grown more intense in recent years, there has been a tendency for the biblical story to be ignored or suppressed in schools, colleges, universities, and the like. A corollary of this development is a decrease in the number of people outside and inside the Church who have even the most basic familiarity with the Biblical narrative. This, in turn, makes communication of the gospel more difficult, as many people do not have enough familiarity with the Christian story to permit them to understand and respond to the gospel. Furthermore, many inside the Church have either forgotten the story of the Bible or never knew it. [32]

To counteract all this, Christians must remember that Christianity survived the end of the Roman Empire and the Middle Ages. It will survive the end of the modern world. Christian faith has a response to the postmodernist critique. Christianity was not founded by a conqueror in a bid for power. The gospel is the story of a God who forsakes perfection, pleasure, prosperity, and power, endures suffering on behalf of humanity, dies a terrible death on the cross, and rises from the dead to reach into human history with unimaginable self-giving love. At our best, Christians do not believe in religious imperialism by which every human being is compelled to believe in Christ. Instead, Christians fundamentally believe that by reaching out in love and service to others and sharing the Gospel, people will, without compulsion, respond by the power of the Holy Spirit to the call of God to live lives of wisdom and love.

— CHAPTER 3 —

Costly Discipleship

The remedy for the predicament of the modern world is counter-intuitive for many Christians and their leaders. Ultimately, the church cannot accommodate its way to better disciple-making and service to our culture. We cannot use the things destroying our culture to save it. Christians can only minister effectively by recovering a more profound, more authentic way of following Jesus, forsaking the easy approaches of cultural accommodation. It will take work.

Before the Second World War, a young German theologian, Dietrich Bonhoeffer, published a book often known as *The Cost of Discipleship*. [1] The thesis of his book was prophetic. Bonhoeffer believed the Christian church in the West had too long preached and dispensed Cheap Grace. This was a terrible mistake. "Cheap Grace," he said, "is the deadly enemy of our Church." [2]

The Problem of Cheap Grace

Bonhoeffer compared "cheap grace" with "costly grace." Costly grace is the grace Christ speaks of when he says, "If anyone would come after me, let him deny himself and take up his cross and follow me" (Mark 8:34). Cheap grace is the offer of forgiveness of sins in a way that costs a believer nothing and requires no faithful response. Bonhoeffer describes cheap grace as "preaching of forgiveness without requiring repentance, baptism without church discipline, Communion without confession, absolution without personal confession. Cheap grace is grace without discipleship, grace without the cross, grace without Jesus Christ, living and incarnate." [3]

On the other hand, costly grace elicits a response of obedience and cross-bearing in a broken and needy world. Costly grace evokes in a believer a life lived in trustful reliance on the grace and mercy of God. Costly grace empowers a believer to see the world as God sees the world and respond as God responds in Christ. Bonhoeffer took up his cross and followed Jesus to martyrdom near the end of the Second World War. [4]

When a church, denomination, or Christian group dispenses cheap grace, it dispenses God's promise of forgiveness and new life, like soda from a fountain at a child's birthday party or beer from a keg at a college fraternity party. All one experiences is a temporary high followed by a hangover. The church today is suffering that hangover from an excess consumption of cheap grace. Too often, the Gospel is presented without recognizing the new life and new form of life offered in Christ.

Discipleship characterized by cheap grace makes a mockery of what God did in Israel's history, what Christ did on the cross, and how committed disciples have lived the Christian life throughout history, sometimes in danger and persecution. Unfortunately, in one form or another, the gospel of Cheap Grace is too frequently the gospel of Western religious groups. [5]

Real grace is a "costly grace." Bonhoeffer likens costly grace to the "Pearl of Great Price" Jesus describes in one of his parables (Matthew 13:44-46):

> "Costly grace is the treasure hidden in the field; for the sake of it, a man will go and sell all that he has. It is the pearl of great price to buy, which the merchant will sell all his goods. It is the kingly rule of Christ, for whose sake a man will pluck out the eye which causes him to stumble; it is the call of Jesus Christ at which the disciple leaves his nets and follows him." [6]

As the saying goes, "Grace may be free, but it ain't cheap." A person who confesses their sins to God, repents (turns away from sin), turns to God with everything they are and possess, takes up their cross in obedience to Christ and his teachings, and lives a holy life in response to what God has done, is a person who has experienced true grace. Grace does not leave us as we are. Grace changes everything. A transformed life is the only response to a human encounter with real, true grace.

Cheap Grace Today

If, in Bonhoeffer's day, cheap grace was a problem for Christian witness, the problem is exponentially more significant in the contemporary Western church. Western churches, and especially American churches, are addicted to cheap grace. In church after church, in sermon after sermon, in Bible study after Bible study, God's love, forgiveness of sins, and redemption in Christ are preached, without emphasis on God's judgment on corruption, the new life into which Christ calls disciples, and the costly road believers must follow. Building strong disciples is nearly impossible if difficult passages and the cost of the gospel are ignored or explained away. [7] The result is, and always will be, a weak, declining, impotent, and declining Christianity.

Christ's Command to Make Obedient Disciples

Jesus' last act was to commission his disciples, saying:

> "Therefore, go and make disciples of all nations, baptizing them in the name of the Father, Son, and the Holy Spirit, and teaching them to obey everything I have commanded. And surely, I am with you always, to the very end of the age."
>
> (Matthew 28:19-20)

The Great Commission was Jesus' last word and directive to his disciples, then and now, to carry out God's program of salvation and new life Jesus initiated during his earthly pilgrimage. Jesus commissioned his followers to make disciple-making the supreme goal of the church. It is the reason for its existence. Jesus has the same plan for the church today at the beginning of the emerging postmodern age.

Making disciples involves being a disciple, having a heart for people, going to where lost people are, helping people enter the life-transforming fellowship of the Father, the Son, and the Holy Spirit, and teaching new believers about the things of God, helping them respond to God's grace by living a God-pleasing life. This kind of discipleship is not something for just incredibly dedicated believers to do while everyone else watches and applauds. Discipleship and disciple-making are for all Christians.

Who is a Disciple?

The Greek word we translate, "disciple," refers to one who learns from another person. Discipleship, however, is not just about learning information. Christian discipleship involves learning a new way of life. Therefore, Christians best learn about God and wise living through a personal relationship with God in Christ, the Bible, teachers, and mentors, and by observing and internalizing the words and actions of fellow Christians. Discipleship involves a life-transforming relationship with a person—The Triune God revealed in Jesus Christ. Just as God exists in relationship, so Christ-followers must live and breathe within a web of healthy relationships to grow as disciples.

Christians proclaim Jesus Christ is "the Way, the Truth, and the Life." In other words, the key to abundant living is not an idea but a personal relationship with Christ through which we are transformed into the likeness of the One who is the Way, the Truth, and the Life. More than head knowledge is required. To know the Way, the Truth, and the Life of Christ, we must become imitators and obedient followers of Christ. As the New Testament says, "Christ must dwell in us richly" (Colossians 3:16).

Because being a disciple involves a relationship with a person, we trust that person and spend time in loving fellowship with that person. Being a disciple is like being a professional athlete or a scientist. A person who admires professional athletes or scientists but never enters into a relationship of learning and emulation is neither an athlete nor a scientist. At most, such a person is an interested onlooker. Authentic disciples observe, emulate and become like the one they are learning from and into whose image they are being conformed (Romans 8:29).

Christians do their best and live wisely with love when we emulate Jesus Christ, allowing his divine life to permeate our entire being. It is not enough to proclaim that we believe in Christ or to bring people to declare their intellectual belief that Jesus Christ was the Son of God. To be a disciple is to follow Christ daily, become more like Christ daily, and help others become more like Christ. Christians are called to support others as they seek to live with the same integrity and self-giving love that characterized Jesus when he ministered to his disciples. This means incorporating the same divine wisdom and steadfast love that characterized Jesus of Nazareth into our lives. It even means being willing to suffer for the gospel as Christ suffered for the human race.

An abstract understanding of knowledge characterizes the modern world from which we are emerging. In our world, God and other people are too often seen as objects to be studied and mastered, not persons to be loved and cherished. Knowledge is measured by tests and one's ability to answer questions, write essays, and regurgitate information. The object is mastery of a subject and increasing control over reality. To the modern mindset, knowledge that is not "scientific" or "objective" is not real knowledge. Wisdom is different. To be wise, one must know some information; however, more importantly, wise people apply and embody information in everyday life.

The earliest name for Christians was "people of the Way" (Acts 19:23, 24:22). To be a "way" is to be a path, road, highway, or boulevard that must be traveled on. Christian faith and discipleship are fundamentally a way of life, a path of wisdom, a road that leads to life, a highway to a better relationship with God, a boulevard to holiness, an embodied knowledge of God. [8]   It is not an event; it is a life-long process of abiding in Christ and allowing Christ to abide in us.

Because the Way is a path we travel, the information we possess, and the rules we master are only a means to an end. The end is becoming more like Christ in faith, hope, and love. The test of whether we are good or bad disciples is found in how we live and what kind of people we are in the depths of our being. This knowledge can only be gained in a community of faith that is surrendered to Christ, dependent upon his grace, abiding in his love, and always and forever empowered by the Holy Spirit.

The Community of Jesus

Jesus did not just preach, teach, and do signs and wonders. Jesus brought people into a human relationship and spent his earthly ministry with the people he was discipling. Other religious figures wrote books. As the missiologist Lesslie Newbigin said, "Jesus did not write a book but formed a community."[9]   Christ chose twelve ordinary people and lived in a relationship with them during his earthly ministry. He also lived in close fellowship with a larger group of men and women with whom he shared his life and teachings (Luke 8:1-3; 10:1; 14:25). Their memories of him are contained in the New Testament. Their memories of Jesus and their time together in a discipling relationship propelled them to carry the Good News of his life, death, and resurrection on a continuing journey to the ends of the earth as they understood it.

Jesus said, "Where two or three come together in my name, there I am with them" (Matt. 18:20). If people are to meet Jesus, a group of people (disciples) must introduce potential disciples to him in a community where "two or more are gathered," a relationship in which Christ is present by the Holy Spirit. If new Christians are to understand what it is like to be a Christian, they need personal mentoring by people who are further along the path of discipleship. [10]   Jesus did not stop making disciples when he ascended into heaven. He continues to do so in every age through communities who are in a relationship with him.

The way the early church grew was by reproducing in community and individual lives who Jesus was and what Jesus had done while he was with his disciples. [11]   The book of Acts is the story of how, by the power of the Holy Spirit, the disciples lived as Jesus lived, did the kinds of things Jesus had done, and faced the same opposition and suffering Jesus faced. [12]   This should be the experience of the church today.

The best way for the Kingdom of God to grow is by ordinary men and women bringing people to Christ, calling them into an authentic community, growing in discipleship together, and training new believers who enter the fellowship "to obey all Christ commanded." Such a community continually reproduces this process through wise and loving outreach, bringing Christ into the lives of those they contact. In all of this, the people of God humbly remember that the Spirit whom Christ promised is the primary agent in their disciple-making.

CHAPTER 4

The Way of a Christ Follower

For most of my life, I had few, if any, hobbies. Just now, I play golf. Here is how it happened: Many years ago, a friend asked if my brother and I would like to play a few holes of golf. We did. In High School, we played a few rounds of golf with friends. This stopped when I went away to college. For years, I rarely played. Then, my wife took a lesson or two just after retirement. Later, another friend invited us to play a round. We liked the game, took a few lessons, and now frequently play golf together. My life was changed by an invitation to spend time on the golf course with friends.

My golf experience pales in importance to another experience. In 1977, I was a lonely young lawyer in a large law firm in a strange city. I had drifted from our family's Christian faith. One Friday evening, a woman at the law firm invited me to attend a Bible study. A few months later, I renewed my Christian faith. In that Bible study, I made life-long friends, experienced the Christian faith firsthand, and was first allowed to develop my teaching gifts. I met my wife in that small group. What we called the "Friday Night Bible Study" profoundly changed my life. I love to read, but the most profound change in my life did not begin with a book. It started with an invitation. It did not begin with an idea. It began with a person.

Jesus Invited People to Become Disciples

The Biblical records that Jesus began his ministry by inviting disciples into a personal relationship with him. Matthew describes it like this:

> As Jesus was walking beside the Sea of Galilee, he saw two brothers, Simon called Peter and Simon's brother Andrew. They were casting a net into the lake, for they were fishermen. "Come, follow me," Jesus said, "and I will send you out to fish for people." At once, they left their nets and followed him. Going on from there, he saw two other brothers, James, son of Zebedee, and his brother John. They were in a boat with their father Zebedee, preparing

their nets. Jesus called them, and immediately they left the boat
and their father, and followed him.

(Matthew 4:18-22)

Jesus found Peter, Andrew, James, and John as they went about their ordinary
day-to-day lives. He did not say, "Stop what you are doing for a few moments
and accept me as your Lord and Savior before going on with your life as before."
He did not ask for an intellectual commitment: "Recognize I am the Son of God,
then you can go back to living the way you did before." He did not ask them to
read his latest book. He said, "Come, follow me."

Jesus asked his disciples for a commitment involving more than their minds.
He asked for a break from the past that involved physically following him. He
might as well have said, "Stop what you are doing. Leave your accustomed life.
Leave the books you are reading right where they are. Stop going to your thera-
pist. Make your hobbies, families, and work secondary. Come and follow me for a
while and see what happens."

It is precisely at the point of an invitation to "come and see" that discipleship begins (John 1:39). In the beginning, the disciples hoped Jesus would be the
politico-military Messiah Jewish tradition anticipated. They had no real idea of
who Jesus was or what he had come to do. Nevertheless, they left their nets and
followed him. The same is true of most of us—we begin the life of discipleship
not fully aware of where it will take us and with a good bit of misunderstanding
of God and his purposes.

Contemporary people often overlook that the disciples entered into **a relationship** right at the beginning of their discipleship, before they knew exactly
who Jesus was or acknowledged him as the Christ. Bonhoeffer puts it this way,
"In the gospels, the very first step a man must take is an act which radically
affects his entire existence." [1]   The beginning of discipleship is following Jesus.
The result is a new relationship and a gradual change of life.

Discipleship as a Life Commitment

Too often, people think of commitment to Christ in intellectual terms, as if
recognizing who Jesus is makes a person a Christian, after which discipleship begins. In evangelism and discipleship, we often ask people to make a verbal statement of faith and say a prayer. We ask them to confess with their lips, forgetting
that they must also believe in their hearts, the center of their very being (Romans
10:9). [2]   We ignore the kind of living relationship that results in life-transforming faith.

When one believes something, that "something" makes a practical difference in day-to-day life. Christians follow Jesus where he leads, in a relationship in which the artificial division between faith and works is overcome. The Gospels remind us that those who believe trust and obey. [3] In John's Gospel, Jesus puts it this way: "Anyone who loves me will obey my teaching. My Father will love them, and we will come to them and make our home with them. Anyone who does not love me will not obey my teaching" (John 14:23-24). To be transformed by the love of God is to become an obedient child of the Father. To be a disciple is to be a follower of the one who embodies the wisdom and love of God in human form.

Jesus wanted his disciples to know who he was, even though they did not fully understand until after his death and resurrection. The key to the disciples attaining that knowledge was to have a personal relationship with the God-Man Jesus. Jesus knew it would take commitment on his part and theirs. He knew they would have to learn to trust him in all of life. He knew that discipling a group of ex-fishermen, tax collectors, and the like would take time. Jesus wanted them to spend time with him, follow him around, hear his teachings, observe his responses to situations, and experience his leadership so that they could become more like him. Therefore, his first act was to invite them into a life-changing personal relationship.

Deciding to Follow Jesus

We sometimes think it was easier for the first disciples to follow Jesus. We believe that if we physically saw Jesus, if he came and personally asked us to follow him, we would find it easier to follow than after hearing a pastor, evangelist, or friend share what God has done in their lives and ask us if we are ready to follow Jesus. [4] This is a mistake. People today have to make the same decision the first disciples made. We must decide to follow Jesus without knowing precisely who he is or where he will lead us.

The first disciples had it just as hard as we do. They had families. They had friendships. They had occupations. They already had a religion. They went to the Temple periodically, made sacrifices, and attended festivals. They probably went to the little synagogue in Capernaum. They had homes and responsibilities. They did not have the gospels or the records of Jesus' life, death, and resurrection that we can read and study. They had much less information than we have.

One day, a man approached them and asked them to follow him and become fishers of human beings. At that moment, they had to decide whether to follow or not. The gospels tell us that the disciples heard the invitation, left what they were doing, and followed (Matthew 4:20; Mark 1: 18, 20; Luke 5:11). Somehow, amidst the hustle and bustle of earning a living, caring for spouses, parents, and children, and being engaged in family and civic affairs, the disciples saw something important in Jesus and decided it was worth the risk of following him into the unknown.

They did not have it easier than we do. They had it harder. We can look back at the generations of lives changed, of people healed, of ministries and missions of compassion and care. We have examples of people like St. Francis of Assisi, Dietrich Bonhoeffer, Mother Teresa, and hosts of others. We have many reasons to know what God can do with one ordinary life.

When Jesus called the disciples, the cross, resurrection, and spreading of the gospel, the church's birth, the example of the martyrs, the evangelization of the world had not occurred. It was all to come. The first disciples had to decide to follow Jesus without any of this history. They were the first followers. They had to look into an unknown traveling rabbi's eyes and answer, "Will I follow him or not?"

We are called to answer the same question: "Am I going to follow Jesus?" As we ponder that question, we ask ourselves the same questions the disciples must have: "Am I willing to follow Jesus and trust him in all my daily life?" "Am I willing to give up everything to be a follower of Jesus?" "Am I willing to spend time with this teacher and his rabble band of followers?" "Am I willing to risk the life I know so well for a life of uncertainty?"

When we ask another person if they are ready to become a Christian, we must be careful not to make it sound too easy. We probably should not say to people, "Are you ready to **accept** Jesus as your Lord and Savior." We should say, "Are you willing to **trust and follow** Jesus in all of life?" Eternal life, the forgiveness of sins, membership in the family of God, and citizenship in the kingdom of God depend upon our willingness to follow Jesus, not tell people we intellectually believe Jesus was the Son of God.

Jesus wants Imitators, not Admirers

The Christian philosopher Soren Kierkegaard reminds us that Jesus does not want admirers—he wants imitators. [5] In ancient times, a disciple was more than just a learner. A disciple followed his master and imitated his master. While learning is a part of a disciple's life, it is not the end or goal of discipleship. Jesus asks us to follow him because he intends us to become little Christs, living as he lived and doing the same things he did. A follower of Jesus will have specific characteristics, the most important of which is that followers of Jesus try to become like Jesus. In becoming like Jesus, we believe we become more like God. Our goal, as the Eastern Orthodox put it, is "theosis," being changed by the Spirit into people filled with the life of God.

Christian faith is not simply objectively knowing who Jesus is, memorizing a few Bible verses, and learning three or four theological ideas. Christianity is a complete way of life initiated by faith and powered by grace. Furthermore, it is a way of life patterned after the life, death, and resurrection of Jesus. It is a life of unconditionally loving others, being a servant, sharing life with others, discovering and using our spiritual gifts, healing our broken world, and speaking truth into the darkness of a world too often governed by lies.

Being a Christian also means learning to bear a cross now and again because the love of Christ bids us bear that cross. This is why Jesus says if anyone would be my disciple, let him deny himself, take up his cross and follow me" (Matt.10:16-24; Mark 8:34; Luke 9:23). If we want to be a disciple of Jesus, we must learn to follow him wherever he leads. We cannot be a disciple any other way but by following Jesus, watching and listening to Jesus, and acting like Jesus. This is what it means to be a disciple.

Counting the Cost

A dangerous failure of churches today is a lack of understanding that the gospel is not primarily a system of doctrine, a theology of grace, or a verbal formula and mental acceptance of propositions about God expressed in a creed, confession, or theological position. Christianity is not just doctrine. The gospel is a way of life. The word we translate as "Faith" can also translated as "Trust."[6]   Faith is seen in trusting and following Christ and responding faithfully to the pressures of daily life. Authentic faith is seen in disciples who follow Jesus regardless of the cost, personally, professionally, or otherwise. Genuine faith is seen in a life-transforming relationship with the living God.

During the Reformation, guarding against the idea that one could be saved by merely obeying a theological authority or doing specific liturgical actions was important. The Reformation was a corrective to the excesses of the Middle Ages. [7]   Today, however, there is a need to correct the false notion that faith is accepting a proposition about Jesus, getting an admission ticket to heaven punched, and then living as before based on a Cheap Grace that does not require change, growth, service, or sacrifice. In other words, if cheap grace was a problem in Bonhoeffer's day, it is a worse problem today.

The call to be a disciple is an invitation to follow Jesus in the daily business of life. It is a call to commit oneself to God in such a way that we follow Jesus, learn from Jesus, imitate Jesus, and grow to become more like Jesus. It means giving our lives, families, careers, hobbies, and social circle to God, and most importantly, includes cross-bearing. To do this, we have to spend time with Christ.

Learning to Bear a Cross

Jesus said, "Whoever wants to be my disciple must deny themselves and take up their cross and follow me" (Matthew 16:24). We cannot be disciples without becoming like Jesus and being willing to experience what Jesus experienced, pleasant and unpleasant. We cannot become like God unless we are willing to give our lives for others in self-giving love. This involves periodic cross-bearing.

Crosses are not difficulties or natural consequences of our behavior and choices. Crosses are decisions we make to suffer for the benefit of others, although we are not required to suffer by law, divine compulsion, or some inner brokenness. Jesus went to the cross because God loves us and sent Jesus to bear our sins and brokenness on the cross because of that love. Being a disciple means taking the sins, shortcomings, and brokenness of others, loving them unconditionally, and accepting whatever inconvenience is required to help them grow in Christ. [8]

Years ago, I was a young lay leader in a large congregation when a serious problem arose. My closest friends, those with whom I was theologically most in sympathy and with whom I wanted to side, were not adopting the best or most godly strategy. On the other hand, members of my own family were on another side of the dispute, whose proponents were not always acting appropriately. It was the first time as a Christian that I had to go against the very people who were most important in my life and Christian walk. It was a time of intense personal suffering. During this time, God taught me an important lesson: Being a disciple does not exempt us from being misunderstood, misquoted, slandered, or deeply hurt. Sometimes, this will happen when doing our most important work for Christ.

To be a disciple is to bear a cross from time to time. I've been a pastor for over twenty-five years and a Christian for more than four decades. Every pastor and Christian leader knows that following Jesus does not exempt a person from suffering and carrying a cross in the name of Jesus. I sometimes say, "Every time God desires to do something important in this world, someone must carry a cross."

The Role of Faith

From the beginning, Jesus warned his disciples what belief in him meant. Mark begins his gospel with Jesus proclaiming the good news and telling his hearers to "repent and believe" (Mark 1:14). The "repent" part means "change" or "turn your life around." The faith of which Jesus speaks is more than knowing Jesus is the Christ. Faith involves turning away from the past, moving out into the future, and trusting in the wisdom and love of God. Faith requires that we give up our self-trust and selfish ambition. If we believe in Jesus, we turn away from the life we lived in the past and begin to live based on the new life we have in Christ. If we have faith, we trust Jesus, move out in reliance on God, and live like Jesus, trusting that a life of loving service to others is the best way of life.

In Galatians, Paul defends the priority of faith. He teaches that we cannot earn our salvation. We cannot be justified by moral behavior or by following the moral law (Galatians 2:16). However, Paul also goes on to say,

> I have been crucified with Christ, and I no longer live, but Christ
> lives in me. The life I now live in the body, I live by faith in the Son
> of God, who loved me and gave himself for me.
> (Galatians 2:20)

Responding to the cross means dying to self and selfish desire ("I have been crucified with Christ"), then living by the power of the Spirit of Christ ("it is no longer I who live, but Christ who lives in me"). Faith means responding by giving our whole selves to God, turning away from our selfish, self-centered ways, and living out of the power of the Holy Spirit.

Faith inevitably involves doing something, living in a particular way, taking specific risks, and acting differently from others. We all have something we must do when we follow Jesus. It is why in Ephesians, Paul says:

> For it is by grace you have been saved, through faith—and this is
> not from yourselves, it is the gift of God—not by works, so that no
> one can boast. For we are God's handiwork, created in Christ Jesus
> to do good works, which God prepared in advance for us to do.
> (Ephesians 2:8-10)

Our works do not save us; however, when we believe in Jesus, we do things we never would otherwise have done because we are different people. We are more loving, more caring, more just, wiser, and more truthful than before. God does not save us because of our works; he saves us so we can become like him. When we become more like God in Christ, we live like Jesus and do the works Jesus did. The reason is not our virtue—it is the power of God working by grace in our lives.

Trust/Faith as a Journey into Change

The Bible tells many stories of faith lived out by faithful people. One of the first of these stories involves Abraham. God told Abraham that he would be the father of many nations if he followed God to the land of the promise (Genesis 12:1-3). Abraham believed and went. In other words, Abraham trusted God not just with his mind ("OK, God, I know you can do this") but also with his heart, soul, mind, body, and strength ("OK, God, I trust you, and I will go"). Abraham followed God in the wilderness for years because of this faith. As James reminds those who think faith can be divorced from works, Abraham's faith was completed by his works (James 2:14-26). A faith that does not change how we think, live, act, and feel is no faith.

When Jesus says, "Come and follow me," he means what he says. He wants us to follow him because we believe he holds the secret to our becoming the people we were created to be. The journey of faith leads us somewhere. Our faith is shown in our discipleship. The person who believes one thing and does another can never be psychologically whole. Our hearts, minds, souls, and spirits must be one to achieve integrity and wholeness.

On the other hand, faith does not change us all at once, as if by magic. The life of faith is a life of slow transformation. During the life of faith, we are slowly but surely made whole as we gradually become the people we profess and want to be. As what we believe in our minds becomes embedded in our hearts, our emotions and behavior change. It is the work of grace we call "sanctification." Sanctification is the process by which what we believe and how we live become one thing in one life.

Just as Abraham went on a journey with God and was changed into a new person, and the disciples went on a journey with Jesus and were changed, when we become Christians, we begin a journey of faith that changes us. It is a journey of following Jesus through a process of discipleship and spiritual growth. It means following Jesus where Jesus goes, with companions (other disciples) who are also following Jesus. It means asking Jesus into our hearts daily through prayer. It means doing what Jesus did and is doing in the world. It means making mistakes along the way, just as the disciples made mistakes, correcting them, and growing along the way. As with any journey, there are twists and turns, blind alleys, and mistaken paths.

A few years ago, a friend and I walked a few days of a pilgrimage on the El Camino de Santiago. The correct path is marked with the sign of seashells. Occasionally, one can miss a marker when the path is not clearly marked. When that happens, it is easy to take the wrong way and have to retrace your steps. That's what happened to us late on the fourth day when we were tired and ready for the day's journey to be over. We had to walk back a mile or so to where we left the path and begin again. The same thing happens over and over on the journey of following Jesus.

We cannot always clearly see Jesus or where he is leading us. Sometimes, the way is obscured. Occasionally, our culture's "thorns and thistles" make the way hard to see. Sometimes, we misread the signs God has given us in Scripture or the advice of others. When that happens, we retrace our steps (ask for forgiveness and make amends), find where we went off the path, and begin again.

God, in His mercy, knows we need instruction, examples, and mercy on the journey of discipleship. At the same time, God brings us safely through the journey because of his steadfast love. This is why Paul could confidently say,

> "I am sure of this, that he who began a good work in you will bring it to completion on the day of Jesus Christ."
>
> (Philippians 1:6)

When Dietrich Bonhoeffer speaks of "Costly Grace," he speaks of a costly grace that transforms and molds us into new beings. Divine grace never leaves us where we were before we received it. Instead, grace bids us to come and die to self with the crucified Christ so that we may be raised to a new and different life by his resurrection power. Grace requires more of us than mere recognition of who Jesus is. It requires that we unreservedly commit our lives and futures to God through him and in light of his revelations of God's nature as love.

CHAPTER 5

The Way of Relationship

Many people (myself included) have difficulty visualizing what it is like to have a personal relationship with God. We can visualize personal human relationships, but we can't see God or ask God out for a date, go on a hunting trip, see a movie, or play a game of pickup basketball. God is not like Jesus in his incarnation. The first disciples saw, touched, and spent time with Jesus. We cannot physically follow the human Jesus of Nazareth around to get to know what God is like. Therefore, it is legitimate to ask the question:

"How can we have a personal relationship with someone we cannot see and who is infinitely different from us?"

The answer begins with bringing ourselves into the presence of God in worship, study, prayer, and other spiritual disciplines. The answer involves joining others in a relationship with Jesus and traveling on the same path in developing a relationship with God in Christ by the power of the Holy Spirit.

A Personal God who Loves Us

Jesus was in a life-transforming relationship with God, other human beings, and God's creation. Jesus calls disciples into that same kind of relationship with him, resulting in a personal relationship with the Triune God, Father, Son, and Holy Spirit. In Jesus, God allows the human race to experience what his "Being in Wisdom and Love" is like in a concrete human life. Jesus asks disciples to spend their lives with him and one another so that they can personally see and experience the wisdom and love of a personal God.

A distinctive characteristic of the Christian faith is belief in a personal God. Christians believe the one God exists as three persons in a relationship of self-giving love. God is Father, Son, and Holy Spirit living in an eternal mutual love relationship. This insight is crucial because it is the foundation of our belief that God is a person and desires a personal relationship with the human race.

The personhood of God is foundational to Christian faith and life. As the early church worshiped, they prayed to and worshiped God as Father, Son, and Holy

Spirit. The earliest liturgies reflect this personal, Trinitarian pattern of worship. The church worshiped, prayed to, and treated all three persons of the Trinity as holy. The idea that God is a person was revealed in Jesus and confirmed by the experience of believers in every age.

As the first Christians heard, wrote, and read about the experience of the disciples (now apostles) with Jesus, they understood that the God of Israel, whom Jesus called "Father," had revealed himself in Jesus of Nazareth, the Anointed Messiah of Israel, who was the "Son of God" and the "Word of God" in human flesh. The church saw that God the Father and Son were present in believers' lives by the Holy Spirit. The names "Father" and "Son" and names like "Spirit of Christ," "Spirit of Jesus," and "Spirit of the Father" indicate that the persons of the Godhead are personal beings, not merely characteristics or forces. [1]

Early Christians worshiped each person in the Trinity as God, a significant barrier to Jewish evangelism and can still be a barrier for people today. To a Jewish person, only God could be worshiped and God is One. The earliest statement of Israel's faith was, "Hear O Israel, the Lord, your God is one" (Deuteronomy 6:4). The question was raised, "If God is one God, how then can we account for Christ and the Holy Spirit?" This resulted in long spiritual and intellectual reflection and a theological debate concerning how the Trinity can be explained. In the end, the church felt that, while there is only one God whom we worship as God the Father Almighty, Maker of Heaven and Earth, this God exists in three persons, the "Father," "Son," and "Holy Spirit." [2]

Personal Relationship and Discipleship

There are many reasons why this is important to discipleship. If God is love (I John 4:8), God somehow has to be a person. Inanimate objects, powers, and ideas do not love. Only people love. In addition, for love to exist, it must be shared. For there to be love, there must be someone (a person) to love and an act of love toward someone else (a person). Dual love, such as between a husband and wife, can be selfish. On the other hand, Triune love involves a degree of unselfishness (as any parent knows). Therefore, it seemed logical to the early church that a God of Love is characterized by unity (One God) and diversity (Three Persons) bound together in a relationship of divine self-giving love—the love Christ revealed to us on the Cross.

We cannot relate to God personally if God is not a person. If God is only a force or a principle, we cannot have a personal relationship with God. At best, we can submit to his power. [3] On the other hand, if God is a person, then there can be a personal relationship between us and God. God can so love us that he would even give himself for our salvation. If God is a person, we can "Love the Lord with all of our hearts, and all of our souls, and all of our minds, and all of our strength" (Matt. 22:35-40; Mark 12:28-34; Luke 10:25-28) and expect that love to be reciprocal. We can love God, and God can love us.

If God is a person constituted by love, the proper and best way to be in a relationship with that God is to reflect God's character, responding to God's love by loving God and God's creation in an earthy approximation to the love that God is. Because God is a person, Christianity is focused on relationships between persons and God, creation, and other people. In other words, faith automatically involves love.

The idea that God must be loved was not new in Jesus' day. In the Old Testament, Israel was to love the Lord with all its heart, soul, and strength (Deut. 6:4-5). This love is to be shown to God and the world (Lev. 19:18). In the Old Testament, God often speaks of his love of Israel. In Hosea, God compares his feelings towards Israel to those of a spouse who has been betrayed (Hosea 3:1). The picture of God's love in Hosea is fundamental because it reveals a personal God who suffers, is humiliated, and yet will not abandon his beloved, however far away the beloved may wander. This love is the same love that caused God to provide in Christ a way for all of us to return to a living, holy relationship with the Triune God.

Persons and Personal Relationships

In our individualistic culture, we celebrate individual personhood, perhaps to excess. Interestingly, however, the modern world has a drastically truncated and vague idea of personhood. We think of a person as an individual, a solitary, discrete body with mind and reasoning powers. This person is bound to other persons by physical and psychological forces (that can be reduced to physical forces) that we can study and come to understand and control. This person is entitled to act as they please as long as they do not harm another person or violate a law.

Human love is often regarded as a complex bio-psychological phenomenon, a biologically-based force acting between persons. We think that love, care, friendship, and other relationships are reduceable to individuals and biochemical relationships between them. When we think this way, people become like living billiard balls—discrete objects careening around, occasionally making contact with other similar billiard balls.

This way of thinking needs to be revised and corrected. Persons are complex, relational beings with minds, bodies, psyches, and spirits. Various physical, mental, emotional, and social life relationships constitute a person. This last part is significant: We would not be who we are without the social connections we experience from the moment we are conceived, which is why the church is essential to growing in Christ.

If modern physics is correct, our bodies are more than material particles bound together by forces. The subatomic "particles" that make up reality are not material. What we call "basic particles" are not material in the classic understanding of that term but "quantized ripples," waves in a field stretching throughout the universe.[4] These quantized ripples are related to one another in such a way that everything in the universe is fundamentally related to everything else. A deep relationality and independent reality characterize such a universe. In such a universe, it should not surprise us that people are profoundly and significantly relational.

When conceived, we are far from an independent reality, unconnected from the rest of the world. Instead, we are composed of the DNA of our parents, unique but dependent upon their entire genetic history. During our gestation, we are connected to our mothers in the most intimate way, enclosed within her body, dependent upon her for our being, sustenance, and life. When born, we are born into a family, not just a biological unit but a social entity with unique characteristics. This family cares for us and provides for us for a long time. We are dependent upon our parents. Who we are and what we become depends on the quality of this relationship. Every relationship we have from that time forward, positive or negative, plays a role in who we become and what kind of person we are.

As time goes by, we enter into relationships with hosts of other people and social groups, each of whom contributes to who we become. Every pastor has seen the terrible harm done to a person when parents and others fail to provide the love, care, respect, and other emotional and physical needs needed in the early stages of life. Such behavior deprives a child of the fullness of human love God intended for that child to experience.

We are born into a community and a culture with unique patterns of life and ways of understanding the world, which form who we are as persons. In addition, the cultures we experience and become a part of during our lives profoundly impact who we are. Anyone who has traveled has experienced the sense that people in other parts of our country and the world live differently and often see things differently than our culture and the people with whom we are the most familiar. I have had the opportunity to travel a lot, and sometimes to the same places more than once. For example, I always recognize that while I love Scotland and my European heritage, nevertheless I am an American, not European or Scottish. Travel both broadens us and reveals the uniqueness of our homeland and culture.

Through all our relationships and experiences, our unique personhood develops. This unique person has the potential for a unique relationship with creation, others, and God. The unique individual has their distinctive physical, emotional, mental, and spiritual being, different from anyone else. Nevertheless, despite our unique personhood, we remain intimately connected to those with whom we have or have relationships.

Every unique individual is called into a relationship with God—the most important, life-changing relationship a person will ever have. Entry into this relationship changes us, just as every relationship changes us. Because this relationship is with the Lord God, the Creator of the heavens and the earth, and all things visible and invisible, we can expect that such a relationship will change us more profoundly than any other relationship.

The Jewish theologian and author Martin Buber spoke about the importance of personal, loving relationships, what he called "I Thou" relationships, with nature, other people and God.[5] Buber begins recognizing that God is not an idea or a principle, of the universe we may know abstractly or entirely objectively, but a person that we know through his creative, revealing, and redeeming acts. God's initiative in revealing God's self as the Divine Person makes it possible and necessary for us to know God as a "Thou."

This is important in understanding why we must have personal relationships with God and others to grow as disciples. It also reminds us that there are limitations regarding how much spiritual growth Biblical and theological knowledge can provide. When our level of abstract ("I-It") knowledge of God, the Bible, theology, etc., exceeds our personal ("I Thou") relational knowledge with the living God, our discipleship stagnates and suffers.

Over and over again in ministry, I have experienced in my own life and the lives of other pastors and teachers the impact of too much abstraction and insufficient interaction with God. Annual retreats, times of silence and solitude, and sabbaticals are essential for Christian leaders because these times build a relationship with God.

Growing a Relationship with God

If God is personal and wants a personal relationship with us, we must ask, "How can we establish and maintain such a relationship?" Although it may seem like an unanswerable question, the beginning step is pretty straightforward:

We have to believe that there is a God who wants a relationship with us.

We have to commit in trust to developing that relationship. If we have faith, then we have a relationship with God. It may be a new relationship. It may be an immature relationship—but there is a relationship. Then, that relationship needs to grow and develop.

Our relationship with God is like any human relationship. If this new relationship is to grow and mature, we must work on it, just as we work on relationships with friends, spouses, children, or co-workers. We have to communicate, which is where prayer comes in. To grow in a relationship with God, we must spend time with God in silence, conversation, sharing, meditation, and growing closer to God. As we trust God and move out in faith, God's wisdom and love are increasingly revealed, and our love grows, even in hard times, just as a good marriage grows in good times and bad times.

When my wife and I were dating, as busy as I was as a young professional, I made time to be with her because I loved and wanted to be with her. We could not spend too much time together. Our relationship grew, and once we were married, our relationship still grew, but the pressure of business, family, church, and activities strained our relationship. We went through difficult times and did not communicate as often or as well, so our relationship suffered. Today, our relationship is still changing and growing. Our relationship with God is similar. It takes time. It has its ups and downs. We cannot take it for granted and must work on it.

Grace and its Emissaries

Christians believe in grace. Grace is God's love reaching out to human beings to form a relationship of mutual love. This relationship is not dependent upon our worthiness. God is always reaching out in steadfast love to relate to human beings. God's love is reaching out to us long before we think about reaching out to God. God's love reaches out to us when we do not sense his presence and believe he might be absent. As Paul reminds us, "In him, we move and live and have our being" (Acts 17:28). God is always reaching out in love.

Of course, if we are to recognize that the invisible God is reaching out to us, it will take another person who already has a relationship with us to tell us about that God and introduce him to us.[6] I had a friend, now dead, who became a pastor a long time ago when it was thought that pastors ought to be married. He went to seminary but never really met the right person. One day, he met a young widow whose husband had died young. He was introduced to her by a friend. My friend might never have met his wife of over fifty years without that friend. Christians are friends who introduce their friends to someone who will meet their deepest needs for love. We must consider ourselves as like my friend's buddy who introduced him to the woman who would be his wife. We do not impose on people when we share God's love. We are introducing them to the best lover they will ever have.

Deepening our Relationship

Worship, Bible study, prayer, and the like are the spiritual equivalent of spending time with and getting to know a human person. To understand what God is like and how to grow our relationship with God, we study our Bibles, Christian literature, and the stories of others who have developed a relationship with God. We pray and spend time with God. We learn to relate to God as a person by reaching out to others in acts of love and mercy.

If our relationship with God is to grow and mature, we also need to spend time with people who are already in a relationship with God, including time with people who have been in that relationship longer and more deeply than we have. We need to be a part of the Christian community and have a relationship with another person or persons who are growing in a relationship with God. Just as we will grow in a marriage if we have friends who are developing a good marriage, our relationship with God will profit from our ability to share our lives with other disciples of Jesus.

A Different Kind of Relationship

Naturally, there will be differences between our relationship with God and our relationships with human beings. We will never physically see God. A lot of the time, God speaks to us in silence. Sometimes we will doubt he is there. No matter how hard we try, we will never fully comprehend the One who is the all-wise, all-knowing, all-powerful Creator and Sustainer of the universe. There will always be mystery and unresolved questions. Occasionally, God will seem silent or absent, as if he has deserted us. We will never control the terms of our relationship with God.

Mother Teresa once led a retreat for a group of married women who complained about the difficulties of marriage. One participant indicated that it would be hard for Mother Teresa to understand the challenges of marriage because she was celibate and unmarried. Mother Teresa replied that she was married to Christ, who could indeed be a very difficult husband!

Like Mother Teresa, we will not always find our relationship with God easy, simple, or without its sacrifices and sufferings.[7]   This is the situation in which Christians find themselves: Faith is a life of relationship with a being (indeed the source of all being) we cannot hope to understand and who, from time to time, may place what we think are impossible demands upon us.

Most of us who have been married any length of time admit to not fully understanding our spouses and believing that they sometimes make impossible demands upon us! Married couples understand that even the best marriages are not always easy. Sometimes our spouses make demands upon us that we frankly believe are unreasonable. Our relationship with God is no different. We will struggle to maintain the relationship and may often wonder what God is up to in our lives. Nevertheless, as the years go by, we grow, and the relationship grows. Its growth is not immediate, constant, or without ups and downs, defeats, and disappointments. After all, on our side, it is a human relationship, subject to the problems with all human relationships.[8]

The Transforming Moment

The life of the apostle Paul is a beautiful example of how God can come into a human life to transform and heal it. Paul was not, as we know, seeking Christ. He was a persecutor of Christ and Christians. Acts tells us that he "held the cloaks" of those who stoned Stephen (Acts 7:58). After that event, Paul violently persecuted the early Christians (Acts 8:1-3).

Having received authority from the Sanhedrin to persecute the church in Damascus, he was met by the risen Christ on the road outside the city. Christ revealed himself to Paul, brought him into a personal relationship, commissioned Paul as a missionary to the Gentiles, and ordered him to go into the city and await his recovery from blindness (Acts 26:12-17). Paul went into the city and was brought into the fellowship of the church in Damascus by Ananias, whose efforts allowed Paul to begin his Christian pilgrimage (Acts 10:7). Paul immediately demonstrated his changed life by his robust defense of Christian faith, a defense he continued to make for the remainder of his life (Acts 9:19-20).

As the example of Paul demonstrates, because God is a person and we are persons, there exists for each human being, however distant from God, the potential for a life-transforming relationship with God, a transformation based upon hearing the Gospel with our intellect, accepting Christ with our hearts, and receiving from God a gracious transformation of our being.

Many years ago, my wife and I met a young divorcee. She was closed to relationships with men and deeply wounded, fearful, and unhappy. Eventually, she remarried. Her new husband was not a Christian. When they had children, the husband decided to go to church. Eventually, he accepted Christ. Later, our friend came to Christ due to her husband's witness. In my former occupation, I used to see this woman from time to time in the tunnels beneath the city of Houston. The next time I saw her after her conversion, instead of seeing her recoil and move away, she broke out into a great smile and came over to greet me. Her relationship with Christ continues to this day. I often reflect on the miracle embodied in the woman's life. I have rarely seen a person so transformed and healed because of a new relationship with God in Christ. This is the power of a transforming, personal relationship with God.

PART 2

LIVE AND LOVE LIKE CHRIST

CHAPTER 6

Sharing Christ's Life

Imagine the scene as Jesus ascended to heaven. Jesus and the disciples had been together for three years. During that time, the disciples formed the belief, hope, and expectation that Jesus was the Messiah who would restore the Kingdom of Israel. They gave up everything and followed him, thinking they would be rewarded when Jesus came to his throne (Mark 10:35-36). Then came his betrayal, arrest, death, and burial. Their hopes and dreams were shattered. Amazingly, three days later, and for several weeks after that, Jesus appeared to them—proving he was alive! Jesus had conquered betrayal, arrest, crucifixion, death, and the grave. They could hardly believe their eyes.

The disciples were now convinced that Jesus, the one with whom they had shared their lives, was their long-awaited Messiah, the true Son of David. Jesus would restore the kingdom of David, just as God promised! (Acts 1:8). But Jesus again surprised them: His physical presence and power would not directly bring in the kingdom. Instead, he would spiritually bring his kingdom into the world through his disciples by the power of the Holy Spirit. Jesus put this new understanding in the form of a commandment or commission:

> "All authority in heaven and on earth has been given to me.
> Therefore, go and make disciples of all nations, baptizing them
> in the name of the Father, Son, and the Holy Spirit, and teaching
> them to obey everything I have commanded you. And surely, I am
> with you always, to the very end of the age."
>
> (Matthew 28:18-20) [1]

In a former congregation, there was a retired pastor who grew up on a farm. He was a southern farm boy. He had been a pastor and a missionary, helping people learn better farming techniques. When he translated the Great Commission, he put it like this:

> "As y'all are going wherever you go, be sure and share the Good
> News with others and make them disciples of mine. As you do this,
> baptize those who come to believe. But don't stop there. Be sure

you teach them all about me and to live the way I have taught you to live. Along the way, don't be scared. I will be with you all the time, everywhere you go." [2]

You have to know a little Greek to understand that Robert accurately captured the essence of what Jesus was saying. In Greek, the word "Go" is a participle. It can mean "Go!" (the imperative form), but it also connotes "As you are going" (the progressive form). Christians are to make disciples (the command) as we go (throughout the progress of our lives). This "country translation" of the Great Commission reminds us that we are always going and should always share God's love and wisdom with others.

Outline of the Great Commission

Because of the importance of the Great Commission, it is vital to get firmly in mind its central principles. The specific task Jesus gave the first disciples and now gives to us cannot be emphasized enough.

- **Go:** Going to church is not what the Christian life is about. The Christian life is about going into the world every day of our lives, including Sunday. We all live and go somewhere every day; where we go and where we are each day is our mission field.

- **Share Good News:** Christians are not simply called to receive teaching. Christians are called to share the reality of Christ and the wisdom and love of God with everyone we meet, not just with people we like. We should communicate verbally and actively through the Christ-like quality of our lives.

- **Make Disciples:** When we have shared our faith and others have accepted Christ, Christians are called to patiently bring people into communities of faith where they can be transformed into the image of Christ. We are not called to make people church members but to make them disciples. [3]

- **Live in the Power of the Spirit:** We do not need to fear. God is and will be with us by the power of the Holy Spirit, the Spirit of Christ, as we share God's love and make disciples. [4]

Making Disciples is More than Words

In the Great Commission, Jesus does not say Christians should "Get people to say they believe in me." He says, "Make disciples" and "Teach them to obey." Too often, evangelism programs stop at conversion. This is not what Jesus asked us to do. He asked us to make disciples who obey his words and teachings and emulate his life through the power of the Holy Spirit. Jesus wants his disciples to be about making more and more Spirit-filled disciples, who live out in their day-to-day lives what they believe in their hearts in such a life-transforming way that other disciples are made along the way.

It is a big job. It requires that we be willing to enter into personal relationships with people, just as Jesus entered into a relationship with his disciples. It means we must put up with immaturity, bad ideas, and hostile behavior, just as Jesus put up with immaturity, bad ideas, and negative behavior. It means that we must be willing to spend time, perhaps years, with others, just as Jesus spent three years or so with his disciples. It means making sacrifices for those we are discipling, just as Jesus made sacrifices for his disciples—even to the cross. Disciple-making involves more than words. It is a commitment and a way of living sacrificially on behalf of other people.

Going While Unqualified

By the time Jesus gave them the Great Commission, the disciples knew they were unqualified for their new duties. During their time with Jesus, they constantly misunderstood him. They did not understand that he would not be a political and military Messiah. They did not understand that he had to be betrayed, tried as a criminal, crucified, die, and be buried. They did not understand that the Good News he proclaimed was for everyone, not just for Jews. At the crucifixion, they all deserted, denied, and betrayed him.

As individuals and as a group, they lacked the character and ability to undertake a worldwide mission. They were not administrators, managers, linguists, theologians, or cross-cultural mission experts. They had neither the education nor the experience to undertake the task Jesus gave them. They could have been more intelligent, gifted, and capable. Nevertheless, Jesus sent them.

Most of us are in the same boat. We don't feel qualified to take the good news to the ends of the earth. We think, "Jesus must have meant to send someone else!" However, he did not. He meant to send the first disciples, and he means to send us. We are in good company if we think we cannot do what Jesus calls us to do. That has been true since the beginning. We are no different from the original disciples if we are afraid, not wholly faithful, and wobbly in our trust in God. To overcome our fears and sense of unworthiness, we must understand that God will be with us by the power of the Holy Spirit if we only go and share.

Taking Time to Make Disciples

One of my favorite New Testament stories is the Twelve's sending on their first mission trip (Matthew 10:1-15; Mark 6:7-13; Luke 9:1-6). After the Twelve had been with Jesus for a time, Jesus sent them out to practice doing what they had seen him do. Mark describes it like this:

> And he called the twelve and began to send them out two by two and gave them authority over the unclean spirits. He charged them to take nothing for their journey except a staff—no bread, no bag, no money in their belts—but to wear sandals and not put on two tunics. And he said to them, "Whenever you enter a house, stay there until you depart from there. And if any place will not receive you and they will not listen to you, when you leave, shake off the dust that is on your feet as a testimony against them." So, they went out and proclaimed that people should repent. And they cast out many demons and anointed with oil many who were sick and healed them.
>
> (Mark 6:7-13)

There is a great deal to learn from this short story: First, Jesus was a master disciple-maker and knew that the disciples would not become the "sent apostles" he needed just by listening to what he said and watching his deeds of power. He did not want them to be just learners but doers as well. He knew they would be on their own someday and needed to prepare for that day. Therefore, he sent them out on practice missions. He did not send them out alone because he knew they would need mutual support. Consequently, he sent them two-by-two.

Second, Jesus wanted the disciples to learn to rely upon God and not upon human beings, even him. Therefore, he carefully told them not to take along a few items that almost anyone would consider necessary. What person leaves on a trip without a suitcase, wallet, a few credit cards, and the like? No one. Jesus knew this and understood that the disciples needed to learn to rely on God's Spirit.

Third, Jesus warned his disciples not to waste time going from place to place but to spend enough time in one place to effectively disciple people. [5] The disciples went as they were told, stayed where they were welcomed, and were excited and energized by what happened. [6]

Making disciples takes time, energy, effort, and patience. We must be willing to live in community with people and teach, mentor, and love each new disciple as they mature in Christ. There will be ups and downs. Some people adapt quickly to the new life in Christ; others take a long time.

Some years ago, Kathy and I were privileged to be a part of a young woman coming to Christ. This particular person did not grow up in a perfect home. Her parents were divorced. Her mother remarried, and her father worked in a profession where he traveled and lived in a distant city. When she gave herself to Christ, she was in an unhealthy relationship.

Today, that woman is an on-fire disciple and disciple-maker—but there were ups and downs along the way! On one notable occasion, our friend failed to tell us about a financial failure on her part. She was evicted from her home on a rainy, cold day. When she came to see me sopping wet, I was as hard on this "daughter in Christ" as I would have been on one of my children! That particular event was a turning point for this person; she has been a constantly growing Christian and mother since then.

Going as Salt and Light

Kathy and I adapted a well-known discipleship technique, from which a book grew, "Salt & Light: Everyday Discipleship." [7] The title comes from the Sermon on the Mount, where Jesus told his disciples:

> "You are the salt of the earth. But how can the salt be made salty again if it loses its saltiness? It is no longer good for anything except to be thrown out and trampled underfoot. You are the light of the world. A town built on a hill cannot be hidden. Neither do people light a lamp and put it under a bowl. Instead, they put it on its stand, where it gives light to everyone in the house. In the same way, let your light shine before others, that they may see your good deeds and glorify your Father in heaven."
>
> (Matthew 5:13-14)

At some point, many of us have been told by doctors to cut down on our salt intake. However, salt is necessary for human life. It is also a seasoning and preservative. Animals and humans need salt to live, and as a seasoning, it preserves and heightens the enjoyment of food. When Jesus says we are to be the salt of the earth, he is reminding his disciples (and us) that they (and we) are to share with others his self-giving, life-transforming love, the most essential thing in the universe. His love is what makes life possible, joyful, and meaningful. Without God's love, life is little more than a struggle. We see the impact of people thinking that life is nothing but a struggle for position, power, and pleasure in our own culture. Living a life of ceaseless struggle is dehumanizing and breaks the human spirit.

John speaks of Jesus as the "true light, which enlightens everyone" (John 1:9). James speaks of God as the "Father of Lights" (James 1:17). John says that "God is Light"—a light in whom there is no darkness (1 John 1:5). Jesus told his disciples that they were "the light of the world." (Matthew 5:14-16). Christians are to walk in the light of God, living wisely and with a deep love for others. Paul says that when we do this, "we shine like stars" (Philippians 2:15). We are to be like a lamp on a table, shining the light of Christ into the room in which it is placed.

The description of God as light, Jesus as the light, and Christians as the living as light reminds us that we must personally embody and experience God's wisdom and love. It is not enough for us to know about Jesus. It is not enough for us to tell others about Jesus. If we do this without growing in Christ ourselves, we become hypocrites and dishonor God. To be a disciple is to shine like Jesus, live in the light of God's presence, be transformed by that light, and share that light with others. In this way, everything we say and do will point others toward Christ and help them experience the wisdom and love of God.

Ministry of Presence

When I was a new Christian, a partner in the firm where I worked gave me an urgent task. The task required a paralegal to complete. As we reviewed the assignment, the paralegal looked over the desk and said, "You're a Christian, aren't you?" She could tell by our conversation that I was a Christian, even though the talk was about filing a document at a particular time in a specific place in Texas. After the paralegal spoke to me, we shared our common faith in Christ for a few moments before going on with the task at hand.

The "going" part of discipleship is not just about going out and sharing Christ in words. It is about living the life of Christ in our day-to-day lives in a way that others take notice even if we say nothing. This does not mean we say nothing. It means that when we say something, the words flow naturally because of who we have become in Christ. When Christians are salt and light, people notice, no matter what words are spoken.

Any pastor who has ever sat at the bedside of a dying person knows that the ministry of presence is one of the most critical ministries disciple-makers have. Some years ago, the father-in-law of one of my elders was in the hospital. I didn't know it, but he was close to death. One Saturday morning, I went to my regular prayer group. On my way home, I decided to visit this person. My job at the time did not involve visitation. Nevertheless, I went. When I got to the room, the elder's wife was sitting with her fragile father. I sat with her for a time and then said a prayer. Later that day, he died.

Before this incident, I was not close to the elder in question. I knew almost nothing about his family. He was not a particularly important supporter. After that event, we were much closer. He became one of the most influential leaders in our church. That morning, I said almost nothing. It was my presence that mattered. The presence of Christians in the lives of those we disciple is one of the essential qualities a good disciple-maker must have. To be a disciple-maker is to be personally involved in people's lives, just as Jesus was personally engaged with his disciples.

Going in Relationship

For their first missionary experience, Jesus sent the disciples out in groups. Our going should involve relationships with others, those *with* whom we minister, and those *to* whom we minister. God desires a personal relationship with us. God also wants us to develop a communal relationship through the church, those with whom God has called to be his special witnessing people to the world. The Christian community is where people come to faith, learn, grow, and put their faith into practice. The church is the place where Christians experience and share a bit of God's kingdom on earth. Therefore, it is no surprise that God wants us to reach out and share what we have experienced in community with others.

Discipleship involves a "triangular relationship." The essence of disciple-making is a life-changing relationship with God, other people, and oneself. This relationship grows in the process of maturity in faith and life.

- First, we have a vertical relationship with the Triune God, the foundation of our Christian life. As we trust God, we enter the community of the Father, Son, and Holy Spirit (John 14:16; 1 John 1:3). This vertical relationship with God changes our inner being and makes us new people. (2 Cor. 5:17).

- Second, just as God exists in a community, we become a part of the community of God and walk with the Triune God in community with other believers. We call this community "the church." Gradually, we become more like Christ, who is the very image of God (Col. 1:5).

- Finally, our inner transformation, grounded in our vertical relationship with God, and our healed horizontal relationships with others, empowers us to reach out to others just as someone reached out to us (I Cor. 15:10; Phil. 2:4).

The life of a disciple is built around all three relationships: We believe in and trust Christ and become passionately in love with God, willing to follow and obey. We are discipled by other Christ-followers as part of a local fellowship of Christians, learning to share our lives as God intended intimately. As we grow, we reach out to our families, communities, workplaces, schools, etc., with the love of God so that others may experience God's wisdom and love. [8] Each of these three movements of faith is important.

Discipleship in an Entangled World

The communal, relational aspect of sharing the Gospel is problematic for contemporary people to understand and appreciate fully. We are accustomed to the radical individualism of our culture and find it difficult, if not impossible, to grasp the necessity of relationships to grow in Christ. If there is a contemporary scientific insight that should change our way of looking at the world, it is the insight that we live in what John Polkinghorne calls "An Entangled World." [9] We live in a world characterized by a deep and fundamental relationality at the most basic level of reality.

Our habitual way of looking at the world as individual entities exercising force upon one another masks a more profound reality—a world of beautiful and elegant relationality, what I sometimes call "Deep Love." [10] The Doctrine of the Trinity, and God's deep, self-giving love characteristic, implies that believers should be in deep, self-giving relationships with God and one another to achieve the wholeness we desire. We cannot be Christians alone because that is not how God lives or wants us to live. It is not the way we were made. We were meant for community. We need to live "entangled" in the lives of others.

The New Testament reveals the communal aspect of the Christian mission. The most famous apostle, and the one about whom we know the most, Paul, rarely traveled alone. He ministered with others. [11] He went on missionary journeys with Barnabas, John Mark, Silas, Timothy, Titus, Luke, and others. At the end of his life, Peter seems to have been in Rome with John Mark (1 Peter 5:13). Paul and John Mark ministered together at the beginning and end of Paul's ministry (Acts 12:25; 2 Timothy 4:11). Paul was a great disciple-maker, but he was not a "Lone Ranger."

The "going" of God's people is a "going in the community." In the modern world, perhaps because of our emphasis on individualism, we idolize those who go alone or seem to go alone on a mission. We celebrate Billy Graham but forget George Beverly Shay, Cliff Barrows, and the hundreds of others who ministered with the great evangelist over the years. We celebrate Mother Teresa but forget the members of her order. We celebrate famous pastors and forget the staff members who make their ministries possible. The fact is that everyone ministers in the community, whether they (or we) know it or not.

Our call to go is not a call to go alone. It is a call for the entire Christian community to go. [12] A few go as individuals, but most will go as a group with support and courage that only a group can muster. The same is true of us today. While a few of us may be called to a solitary mission, most of us will go as a part of a team. Some will go far away, but most will go to their prior community.

The Lost Art of Going

When I began writing this book, I reread Dietrich Bonhoeffer's *Cost of Discipleship* after many years. I examined the bibliography to look for references to the Great Commission. There were none. The only reference in my edition to Matthew 28 related to the presence of the Holy Spirit with believers and was part of the chapter on baptism.[13] In the late 1930s, writing as a German, a citizen of the home place of the Reformation and the center of Christian Europe, Bonhoeffer could not fully see the need for the church as a community to recommit itself to evangelism and disciple-making.

This omission is a legacy of the fact that, when the Reformation occurred, Germany and all of Europe were already Christianized. The great age of disciple-making, extending for hundreds of years after Jesus' death and resurrection, was thought to be over in Europe. Europe in the early 20th century might not have been a good example of Christianity, but it was nominally Christian. Although by the end of his life, when he was writing to his family and friends from prison, Bonhoeffer could see that Christianity in Germany and Europe was in a crisis, at the time of *Cost of Discipleship*, he could not see the problem.[14]

Many Christians in the United States today fail to see that we are not only in a postmodern era but also in a post-Christian age. Christian faith cannot live on its prior religious or cultural achievements as impressive as they are. Instead, Christians must reach out and share the Good News Christ has entrusted to us. We must recover the lost art of going and sharing the Gospel, or the discipleship crisis will continue and worsen.

Going and making disciples is no longer the responsibility of a few talented individuals. It is the responsibility of all of us. Just as not everyone who traveled with Paul was a great speaker, not all of us are called to be great speakers. We are called to share our faith as we can in the ways we are most gifted. However, no Christian is completely exempt from verbally sharing their faith when the circumstances require it. What is important is that we share our faith in the way we are called and gifted to do so. More importantly, we are called to invest our lives in others' lives so that people not only believe but become well-taught, well-mentored mature disciples of Christ.

I have been a Christian for the better part of half a century. I've been a pastor of evangelical congregations for a quarter of a century. Only recently did I fully recognize that much of what I have taught and accomplished as a pastor is distant from what God intends for the church. There is nothing wrong with great worship, church music, visitation programs, Sunday School, children's programs, youth groups, sound Bible teaching, men's and women's ministry, community outreach, foreign missions, renewal events, etc. God desires his church to do all these things. However, if we do these things without making and empowering disciples, we fall short of what God wants for us and the world—to make disciples.

CHAPTER 7

SHARING GOOD NEWS

Many (if not most) Christians, even if convicted, that they ought to share their faith either cannot or do not share their faith. Christians attend evangelism or discipleship classes but leave if there is the slightest possibility that they will be asked to share their faith outside the group. This tendency prevents the church from accomplishing the very task for which it was created. The reasons for this failure go to the heart of effective gospel communication:

- People don't know **what** to say in communicating their faith.

- People don't know precisely **how** to communicate their faith.

- People are **afraid** to share their faith.

If contemporary Christians are to overcome the decline of the Christian faith, disciple-makers must address the "what" and the "how" of disciple-making and help Christians overcome their fears. Fortunately, the best way to share our faith with another person is a way that comes most naturally to the person sharing their faith.

Years ago, a business associate and friend, not a Christian, asked me out of the clear blue sky if I felt he would go to hell. He knew I was an earnest Christian and wanted to hear my answer. I had never given the question of my friend's eternal destiny one moment of thought. I was embarrassed and did not know what to say. I stared at him blankly for a few seconds and then gave a halting answer affirming our friendship.

I have never felt good about my answer because I do not think I came close to addressing what was really on his mind. What was most deeply wrong with my response was that I did not communicate the importance of our friendship, personal faith, or my testimony to God's love in a way my friend could understand. Because of my fear, I failed to share God's word of love with another human being. I made a mess of a one-time opportunity. My friend is fine, but I do not feel good about my answer to his profound and important question. He deserved better.

Jesus and the Gospel

Jesus freely and lovingly shared the gospel with people. In Mark, Jesus proclaims that the kingdom of God is at hand at the very beginning of his ministry. (Mark 1:15). Jesus began his public ministry, communicating personally and verbally that the Kingdom of God was present. Therefore, the people of God should repent and believe the Good News (Gospel). A more extended account in Luke gives us additional information about the gospel Jesus proclaimed. If sharing the Good News was important to Jesus, it should also be important to us.

In Luke's Gospel, Jesus begins his career in Nazareth, quoting Isaiah as follows:

And he came to Nazareth, where he had been brought up. And as was his custom, he went to the synagogue on the Sabbath day, and he stood up to read. And the scroll of the prophet Isaiah was given to him. He unrolled the scroll and found the place where it was written,

> "The Spirit of the Lord is upon me,
>   because he has anointed me
>   to proclaim good news to the poor.
> He has sent me to proclaim liberty to the captives
>   and recovering of sight to the blind,
>   to set at liberty those who are oppressed,
>   to proclaim the year of the Lord's favor."

> He rolled up the scroll, returned it to the attendant, and sat down. And the eyes of all in the synagogue were fixed on him. And he began to say to them, "Today this Scripture has been fulfilled in your hearing."

> (Luke 4:16-21)

This passage communicates a good deal about what Jesus means by Good News:

First, the gospel is the fulfillment of the hopes of Israel for a Messiah. The Jewish people were subservient to other nations for most of their history. During that time, they dreamt of release from captivity. As a conquered people, the Jews were poor compared to their Babylonian, Persian, Greek, and Roman captors. They were oppressed and subject to arbitrary imprisonment.

Second, Jesus is the foretold Messiah. The good news is that God came to rescue his people in Christ. Surprisingly, this salvation is not for the wealthy, the powerful, the religiously active, the best followers of the law, or the saintly in the eyes of the world. Instead, it is for everyone, even the poor, the oppressed, the imprisoned, sinners, tax collectors, and a host of others no one expected that God cared about. In other words, the gospel is for everyone.

Third, the Gospel is going to have consequences: People in captivity will be released, blind people will see, and people who are oppressed will be liberated from their oppression. The world and individual lives will be better, whole, joy-filled, and healthy because of the Good News Jesus proclaims and is.

The First Disciples and the Gospel

As they went into the world to share the gospel, the disciples developed different ways to explain the meaning of the life, death, and resurrection of Jesus. The Apostle Paul, perhaps the most effective early missionary, described the gospel differently to his hearers at different times. Near the end of his ministry, writing to Timothy, his beloved helper, he said: "Here is a trustworthy saying that deserves full acceptance: Christ Jesus came into the world to save sinners– of whom I am the worst" (I Timothy 1:15). Embedded in this little sentence is a basic form of the gospel:

- The way to salvation is Jesus Christ, who came to save the human race; and

- Every human being needs forgiveness and new life; and

- I found salvation in Christ.

A more extended version of Paul's gospel occurs in First Corinthians, where he writes:

> Now, brothers and sisters, I want to remind you of the gospel I preached to you, which you received and on which you have taken your stand. By this gospel you are saved, if you hold firmly to the word I preached to you. Otherwise, you have believed in vain.
> For what I received I passed on to you as of first importance: that Christ died for our sins according to the Scriptures, that he was buried, that he was raised on the third day according to the Scriptures, and that he appeared to Cephas, and then to the Twelve. After that, he appeared to more than five hundred of the brothers and sisters at the same time, most of whom are still living, though

some have fallen asleep. Then he appeared to James, then to all the apostles, and last of all he appeared to me also, as to one abnormally born.

(I Corinthians 15:1-8)

In this passage, Paul shares the gospel narratively, answering the historical question, "What happened in Christ that causes me to believe him to be Good News?" He begins by stating the importance of the gospel: It is the source of salvation and renewed relationship with God. Having established the fundamental nature of the gospel, he tells the story of Jesus' death and resurrection. The good news is embedded in the story of the life, death, and resurrection of Jesus.

First Corinthians was one of Paul's earliest letters. Second Timothy was one of the last. In Second Timothy, Paul speaks of the gospel in these words:

So, do not be ashamed of the testimony about our Lord or of me his prisoner. Instead, join with me in suffering for the gospel, by the power of God. He has saved us and called us to a holy life, not because of anything we have done but because of his own purpose and grace. This grace was given us in Christ Jesus before the beginning of time, but it has now been revealed through the appearing of our Savior, Christ Jesus, who has destroyed death and has brought life and immortality to light through the gospel.

(2 Timothy 1:8-10)

Although the context and wording are different, the Gospel is the same: God's appointed savior, Jesus Christ, came to rescue the human race from its alienation and sin. This Christ manifested God's wisdom, love, and power in his life, death, and resurrection. The Gospel provides a means of salvation for everyone who believes in Christ and accepts the gift of the forgiveness of sins and the new life God offers them. This salvation is a matter of God's grace, not human achievement.

Paul does not merely share the content of the Gospel. He also shares its application to him and its importance for his life. The gospel is not good news unless and until it is good news to a person. The various ways that Paul expresses the gospel's content relieves us from the false idea that there is only one way to communicate it. Good communication involves a communicator, a message, and the message's recipient. A good communicator is careful to share the gospel message in different ways with different people in differing circumstances. Exactly what is said depends on the person or persons to whom we are communicating. By the power of the Holy Spirit, Paul did just that.

Postmodern People and the Gospel

What is the best way to communicate the gospel today? People often say, "If it was good enough for Jesus and Paul, it is good enough for me." This is true, but it does no good to speak words to other people that they do not, cannot, or will not understand. Therefore, we need to communicate the gospel to people so that those we are communicating with can hear and understand. This requires that we think about the person with whom we are sharing the gospel and the best way to communicate with them.

Good News from God

In Greek, the word we translate, "Gospel," means "Good News." Before the last few hundred years, there were no newspapers or electronic or other forms of mass communication. When an emperor, king, or person in authority wanted to communicate something important, the communicator used heralds who read and proclaimed what was to be shared. These proclamations were news from their leader. This is the root idea of the Gospel: it is a message of hope and healing from God, the King of Heaven, to all of his subjects, everyone, and everything he had created.

Imagine how crucial good news is if it is news from God. The first apostles were commissioned to transmit the most important good news possible: News from God concerning how humans can find forgiveness of sins and have eternal life. That is why Jesus, the apostles, and the church ever since have used the term "Good News" to describe what God is communicating to the human race in Jesus. The most powerful being in the universe has sent his heralds to proclaim the best news anyone can ever hear! You can have a life-changing relationship with me now and forever. In this life, you can experience release from self-centered captivity to sin and brokenness.

This is the first and most important thing to remember in communicating the Gospel: It is the good news of an essential kind—good news from God that he has brought salvation to his people so that they might be freed to become the people he intended.

Good News for Captives

Although we live in a society of unparalleled freedom, contemporary people continue to be captives to sin, self-centeredness, and brokenness. Such people need the healing and liberating power of God. In some areas of the world, people live in physical captivity, not much different from the captivity of the ancient

Jews. In the West, there is a different kind of captivity. People are captive to cultural brokenness and the personal, social, moral, and spiritual brokenness that our culture creates.

Because modern people are inclined to believe that there is nothing beyond the material universe and that this world's activities, possessions, and pleasures are the only hope for meaning and purpose, many people are held captive to a constant search for money, possessions, power, and pleasure. The result is deep spiritual emptiness. This emptiness leads to anti-social and personally harmful behavior: drugs, promiscuity, uncontrolled greed, abuse of other people, and the like. Into this situation, God sends his disciples to proclaim the Good News.

In our day, false gods are not set up in a temple built in the center of our cities. Our false gods are worshipped in office buildings, school rooms, government offices, mansions, and many other places. The prophets of our false gods are not odd figures running around half-naked and half-mad. Modern prophets, priests, and priestesses of false religion speak through the media, cell phones, mass entertainment, popular music, and education. They are made up to look beautiful, handsome, and attractive, and they pretend to be exhilaratingly happy, though their personal lives often do not bear out their external façade.

We worship the false gods of our day in the fabric of ordinary day-to-day life. Most of the time, we do not even know we are bowing down to an idol. To be raised and educated in the West today is to be raised in captivity to a false and damaging worldview that breaks and hurts nearly everyone. It is captivity to the material world and to material things. To escape this captivity, people need to see and have a relationship with people who have escaped and found freedom, wholeness, and blessing in Christ.

Explaining the Gospel to Postmodern People

About a decade ago, I was in my office late on a Friday afternoon. I got a call from the front desk informing me that a disturbed individual was asking for help. I went up and brought the person to my office. Without going into detail, this person was in a sinful lifestyle, selling her body to men, taking mind-altering drugs, and in a relationship of physical and moral abuse. She was not highly sophisticated and had been drinking heavily. I knew that whatever I said to her had to be simple. The only thing I knew to do was share the gospel in a short form. I took out a piece of paper, drew a little diagram, and shared the essential elements of the gospel. My guest had been raised in a poor, minority church. She knew the story. As I shared the gospel with her, her eyes were filled with tears, and she cried. She prayed for forgiveness. This short sharing of the Gospel was precisely what this person needed. By God's grace, she gave her life to Christ.

I did not set out that morning to bring someone to Christ. I didn't set out to form a relationship with the kind of person who came to my office that afternoon. Nevertheless, I knew just enough to help this woman in distress. Our congregation's help did not end with words: Our church shared with this woman some physical resources she and her child needed. This example is a reminder that words and deeds best convey the gospel. As we share God's love with others, we reveal to them that God is love in a way they can personally experience. As we disclose the love of God to them, we open an opportunity for them to join their life to that God of love. That commitment is the beginning of a life of discipleship.

There are many kinds of gospel presentations. One of the most famous portrays sin as a chasm that separates us from God and the cross as a bridge allowing us to cross over and be reunited with God as we accept God's grace and believe in the gospel. This presentation emphasizes our sinfulness and need for the cross. Another famous gospel presentation contains three pictures, one with me on the throne of my life, one with me on the throne of my life but God somewhat involved, and one with God on the throne of my life. This presentation emphasizes our human pride and desire for self-sufficiency.

When Kathy and I wrote a book about sharing the gospel called *Salt & Light*, we prepared a little graphic that can be meaningful to postmodern people. One characteristic of postmodern people is that they often do not have a sense of sin. Because there is no God and no ultimate truth, there is no place in their thought world to believe that we human beings are in a state of rebellion against God.[1] They are not instinctively inclined to believe that they are "sinners" in need of a savior.

Interestingly, contemporary people do have a sense of brokenness. Our society is characterized by pervasive brokenness and anxiety. Emotional fragility and neurosis are at an all-time high. This situation opens up the door for a new and different way to present the Gospel to people—by focusing on God's love as a healing agent for the fragmentation, anxiety, and loneliness people feel in our culture.[2] Just because contemporary people do not think of themselves as sinners, the explanation that they often have for their unhappiness is that they are broken by past experiences, trapped in unhealthy relationships, and victims of the abusive behavior of others. This requires a somewhat different approach to presenting the gospel.

Here is the graphic we developed:

Apart from God's Love

**Touching God's Love
Once in a While**

**Surrounded by
God's Love**

The graphic begins with the actual situation of people who do not believe in God: People almost always consider themselves far from God's love if they do not believe in God or that God is love, as Christians do. Most non-Christians can get that far. They often feel unloved by their parents, friends, spouses, siblings, and others. In any case, they do not feel unconditionally loved because humans cannot give others the kind of love God provides.

The second image shows what happens when people draw near to God, even occasionally: They are now in contact with God's self-giving, unconditional love. Again, many people who do not believe in God or have not established a relationship with God often have had some experience of calling out to God and being spiritually touched in some way. People who do not believe in God or have little or no relationship with God still call out to God on a battlefield, when a loved one is ill, or when they or someone they know are in danger. Finally, the last panel shows the person inside of the love of God with a relationship with God.

The third image shows a person surrounded by God's love. One of Paul's favorite images is of believers being "in Christ."[3] One of my favorite verses is, "If anyone is in Christ, they are a new creation, the old has gone the new has come" (2 Corinthians 5:17). This "in Christness" of believers is both spiritual and physical, as believers accept Christ and live in Christ and enter the body of Christ, which is the church.

The graphic emphasizes the new life and new way of life people receive as they live "in Christ." Paul means that our position in Christ leads us to become new creations with different ideas, plans, hopes, dreams, and the like. Paul also believes that this new life we receive in Christ puts us into a new place regarding following the teachings of God: We have been freed from our innate inability to achieve holiness and now can live the new life in freedom. The love of God surrounds us, physically and spiritually, and changes our entire being and circumstances.

A Gospel Summary

If we put together all the biblical evidence, the gospel might be described something like the following:

- Because God created and loves the world and everyone in the world and wants an eternal relationship of love with the world and everyone in the world, God is always acting in history to show his love to others.

- The story of Christ is the story of the good news God was and is providing for the human race despite its sinfulness, mistakes, and self-centeredness. That story continues to this day.

- God's transforming love became present in Jesus Christ, through which Christ revealed the extent of God's love on the cross to provide forgiveness for sins and release from guilt, shame, and brokenness.

- We enter a new, life-transforming relationship with God through Christ by believing the promise and trusting in Christ.

- This new relationship frees us to become the people God intends us to be and live a life characterized by faith, hope, and love through which we experience the fruit of the spirit: love, joy, peace, forbearance, kindness, goodness, faithfulness, gentleness and self-control.

- Christ will continue to be with us by the power of the Holy Spirit beyond the moment we accept Christ as he makes us into a new, Spirit-filled, and Spirit-empowered person.

Beyond Gospel Presentations

Some Christians misunderstand the place gospel presentations have in Christian life. Accepting Christ is like being born: It's only the beginning of a new life. Just as a mother would not desert her newborn baby, we must not think our job is over when a gospel testimony has been shared. Sharing, therefore, is not the end. It is the beginning. Every time we share Christ, we move into a discipleship relationship with the person with whom we communicate the love of God. We are to become like a midwife helping a woman deliver a child or a mentor helping a young business person find success. We can't desert our charge because they need us.

One benefit of this approach is that we do not need to feel compelled to share everything we know about the gospel with another person in a single setting. It is impossible to share all that God means by "good news" in one sitting or at one time. The riches of Christ are too vast for that to be possible. As we "teach a new disciple to obey all that God has commanded," we have plenty of time to share aspects of the gospel that we had neither the time nor the ability to communicate when they became disciples of Christ.

Putting it All Together

As indicated above, the New Testament is littered with examples of gospel presentations and descriptions. These various presentations give us an idea of what a good explanation of the Gospel needs to say:

1.   First, any gospel presentation needs to center on Jesus: his life, his death, his resurrection, and his continuing work in the people of God who believe he is the true revelation of the mercy of God.

2.   Second, a good Gospel presentation includes the human need for God—that we are separated from God. We are finite, mortal, and do things we know to be wrong and misguided. For this, we need forgiveness and a new life.

3.   Third, to be good news, a Gospel presentation needs to assure hearers that a wise and loving God has provided us a way to fellowship with Him, the forgiveness of sins, and a kind of life we can only imagine.

If I were to write out a short gospel presentation, it would go something like this:

> *Everyone I know, including myself, sometimes feels alienated from God. We have done things that we know are wrongheaded. We do not necessarily sense the love of God in our lives. The people I know who have tried to overcome their sinful nature by hard work have failed, myself included. Some gave up entirely, and some became hypocrites trying to appear better than they are. What I needed, and what most people want, is inner healing and transformation. God loves us enough to send Jesus to provide us with a way to experience that transformation as we become his disciples. God sent his Son, Jesus Christ, into the world to show us what a wholesome life would be like, teach us God's ways, and die for our sins, showing us the extent of God's amazing grace. God raised this Jesus from the dead, and then he promised to send his Holy Spirit to us when we believe, forgiving us and changing us from the inside out. I have experienced this in my own life.*

One thing is sure: We should not allow ourselves to be unprepared for that moment when we have an opportunity to share the gospel. Every Christian should think about what they will say when the opportunity comes. It will come. If we pray for the opportunity to share with our family, friends, neighbors, co-workers, and others, God will give us that opportunity.

CHAPTER 8

SHARING YOUR TESTIMONY

People misunderstand what it means to testify to what God has done in our lives. Jesus came bearing witness to his relationship with God the Father. Jesus' disciples bore witness to their personal experience of Christ the Messiah. By the power of the Holy Spirit, the disciples testified throughout the known world that they were witnesses to what God had done in Jesus Christ, whom they worshiped as the Son of God (Acts 3:15).

The Way of the Story Teller

The gospel comes to us in the form of a story. The four Gospels are the memoirs of the disciples and others as they remembered their relationship with Jesus.[1] Mark, for example, presents Peter's on-again, off-again status as a follower of Christ and leader of the disciples. Mark, which many believe contains Peter's memories recorded and edited by John Mark, paints the disciples, and especially Peter, as clueless and wishy-washy, not understanding who Jesus was or the true nature of his messiahship. After the resurrection, the disciples were changed and went onto the Roman world, boldly proclaiming Jesus as the world's Savior.

One reason we read the Bible and particularly the gospels, is to remember and be able to tell the stories of Jesus. One reason disciple-makers memorize Bible stories and gospel presentations is to share Jesus's stories with others and bear witness to him. However, there is more to disciple-making than telling stories from the Bible or sharing Gospel presentations. We must be able to tell our stories of what God has done for us.

What is a Testimony?

The word "testimony" comes from the same root word as "witness." The Latin word we translate, "witness," also can be translated as "testify."[2] A witness testifies at trial about matters concerning which they have personal knowledge. Our testimony to Christ reflects our unique experience of God in our lives. Just as an expert witness testifies to matters about which they have expertise, a Christian witness is a witness of things they have come to believe due to their own personal experience, thought, and study.

Testimony at trial is evidence one side or the other submits to the court for consideration to support their case. In the same way, our testimony is evidence for the gospel. Potential Christians weigh this evidence with other evidence, just like a court weighs the evidence submitted at trial. Like almost all evidence, personal testimony is not the whole case. It is just a part of the case. Therefore, Christians don't need to ask too much of themselves in relating their testimony to another person. Christians are only responsible for truthfully testifying about what they have experienced during their walk with Christ.

The Greek word for testimony is also the root word for the English word "martyr." This is appropriate. Everyone fears potential embarrassment and rejection in speaking about debatable matters. Christians understand that there may be push-back against their testimony. People may reject a testimony. Some people may even be offended and angry.

Nevertheless, Christians must die to that fear and anxiety when witnessing Christ. God wants us to have the courage to say what we believe and its difference in our lives. The first disciples had to die to their fears. So do we.

The Importance of Testimonies

In the emerging American postmodern culture, the capacity to share what God has done in our lives is vital. One characteristic of postmodern people is an intense pragmatism about religion and personal choices in general. Because people are not inclined to believe in ultimate truth or goodness, "truth" and "goodness" are often thought to be what works for an individual at a particular time.[3] What is true or good for one person or in one society may not be true or good for another. What matters is, "Does it work for me?" In such a culture, stories of God's impact on a person's life make a tremendous difference to listeners.

People may not believe in God, but they cannot deny the impact an experience of God had on another human being. Our testimony is not a defense of the reliability of the Bible or an argument for the evidence of the gospel. It is the story of what God has done in one contemporary life. People may not believe in Truth, but if they see the difference that the Way, the Truth, and the Life made in another life, they may begin to question their current belief system. Therefore, we should be willing and able to testify to what a difference God has made.

Testimonies of Action

Our testimony is not just what we say. Our testimony includes what we do. As friends, acquaintances, and others watch Christians in business, marriages, family life, social relationships, schools, and other venues; they notice if followers of Christ are visibly wise and loving. They look for signs of hypocrisy. How a Christian lives day-to-day ordinary life can be the most powerful, personal testimony concerning the difference faith makes.

When I practiced law as a young associate attorney, people knew I rarely worked on Sundays. I came in almost every Saturday and worked at least part of the day. However, I never came in on Sunday unless requested by a partner or client. People knew this was because I was a Christian. They knew I needed to be in worship and spend Sundays with my family. They may not have agreed but they knew it was my way of life. In at least one case, another person noticed and was impacted by my behavior. People notice when we demonstrate the Christian way of life in our daily lives.

Testimonies of Words

A lived testimony to faith in Christ is essential. However, this does not mean Christ-followers don't need to share their faith verbally with others. Christians must be able to tell people what God has done in their lives. Just as words without action are insufficient, actions without words are inadequate.

The Apostle Paul told his story to others to bring them to Christ and encourage their faith. His testimony is recorded more than once in Acts and again in Galatians (Acts 22:1-21; 26:4-20; Galatians 1:13-2:21). We can deduce that Paul's testimony was essential to his mission of sharing the gospel. I imagine Paul told his story hundreds of times in many different homes and cities during his ministry.

In Acts, Paul tells his story at length to his fellow Jews. Here is the story as Paul describes it:

> I am a Jew, born in Tarsus of Cilicia but brought up in this city. I studied under Gamaliel and was thoroughly trained in the law of our ancestors. I was just as zealous for God as any of you are today. I persecuted the followers of this Way to their death, arresting both men and women and throwing them into prison, as the high priest and all the Council can themselves testify. I even obtained letters from them to their associates in Damascus and went there

to bring these people as prisoners to Jerusalem to be punished. About noon as I came near Damascus, suddenly, a bright light from heaven flashed around me. I fell to the ground and heard a voice say to me, "Saul! Saul! Why do you persecute me?" "Who are you, Lord?" I asked. "I am Jesus of Nazareth, whom you are persecuting," he replied. My companions saw the light, but they did not understand the voice of him who was speaking to me. "What shall I do, Lord?" I asked. "Get up," the Lord said, "and go into Damascus. There you will be told all that you have been assigned to do." My companions led me by the hand into Damascus because the brilliance of the light had blinded me. A man named Ananias came to see me. He was a devout observer of the law and highly respected by all the Jews living there. He stood beside me and said, "Brother Saul, receive your sight!" And at that very moment, I was able to see him. Then he said: "The God of our ancestors has chosen you to know his will and to see the Righteous One and to hear words from his mouth. You will be his witness to all people of what you have seen and heard. And now what are you waiting for? Get up, be baptized, and wash your sins away, calling on his name." When I returned to Jerusalem and was praying at the temple, I fell into a trance and saw the Lord speaking to me. "Quick!" he said. "Leave Jerusalem immediately because the people here will not accept your testimony about me." "Lord," I replied, "these people know that I went from one synagogue to another to imprison and beat those who believe in you. And when the blood of your martyr Stephen was shed, I stood there giving my approval and guarding the clothes of those who were killing him." Then the Lord said to me, "Go; I will send you far away to the Gentiles".

(Acts 22:1-21)

Paul's testimony has three critical features:

1. First, he tells what kind of a person he was before Christ called him to be an apostle.

2. Second, he tells how this happened in a dramatic encounter with Christ, much as the prophets describe their calling.

3. Third, he tells what happened because of his decision to become a follower of Jesus. [4]

Before Paul became a Christian, he was a persecutor of Christians. He hated Christ and the Christian faith. Then, he met Christ on the road to Damascus, on his way to persecute the Christians in that city. As a result of his conversion, Paul became a missionary to the Gentiles.

Finally, and often missed, is the fact that Paul became part of a community when he received this call: He was taken to Damascus, where eventually he was accepted by the church and ministered to by its members. He was welcomed by the Jerusalem church, though not by everyone (Acts 9:8-19). Later, Barnabas came beside Paul and allowed him to use his gifts in Antioch, from where he was sent on his missionary journeys (Acts 11:25-26). At his conversion, Paul became a part of a Christian community.

In my view, all good testimonies have four characteristics:

- What kind of person I was before I encountered Christ.

- How I met Christ.

- The difference faith in Christ made in my life.

- What community of faith I became part of because of my calling.

Most mature Christians remember how they lived before, how they became Christians, and what changed because they accepted Christ. Most Christians have testimonies of what God has done in their lives and how it changed them. Notice that the story of Paul's Christian experience does not end with his conversion on the Road to Damascus (1:18-2:21). Neither does our calling to follow Christ as a disciple of the Risen Lord.

Dramatic and Nurtured Testimonies

Some Christians hesitate to share their faith story with others because they feel it is not good, powerful, or dramatic enough. This is a big mistake. I have a pretty dramatic testimony of how God came into my life. On the other hand, my wife has been a Christian almost all her life. Her story is less dramatic. It is important to remember that there are as many different testimonies as there are persons, and there is more than one type of testimony. Each of these testimonies is important to someone, and someone will respond to that testimony.

People sometimes talk about the difference between dramatic conversions and nurtured conversions. A dramatic conversion usually occurs when someone has been far from God and is brought close to God in a single theatrical event or series of events. A nurtured conversion usually involves a parent, grandparent, or another significant person who gradually encouraged the believer to be a Christian.

In my case, I was far from God and not looking for Christ when I suffered a series of failures and losses. At a critical moment, a co-worker invited me to a Bible study. Over several months the members of this Bible study nurtured me until I came to believe in Christ. On the other hand, my wife grew up in a Christian family, was cultivated as a Christian by her parents, accepted Christ at an early age, and never strayed very far from the Christian faith or behavior. She can, however, remember various times when God worked in mighty ways and led her toward deeper faith and commitment to Him.

One type of conversion story is no better than another. Most of the time, people have a dramatic conversion story because they were out of fellowship with God in a destructive way. I often say that my more dramatic conversion is not a matter of my great spirituality but my incredible lack of spirituality! Because of my hard-headedness, God knocked me over with a "spiritual 2 x 4" to get my attention! In other words, it doesn't speak ill of you if you don't have a dramatic conversion. It speaks well of you.

We should not emphasize one kind of conversion story as superior because people have different life experiences. A person who is quiet, meditative, and somewhat in touch with God may not have a dramatic experience at all. The story of a calm experience of Christ will significantly impact that person more than a dramatic story. On the other hand, a person who is dramatically out of touch with God may respond to a more dramatic testimony. Every Christian was given their testimony which is meaningful to people like them. Whatever our testimony, we must be prepared to share it with others.

God's Continuing Work in a Life

People love to hear the story of how someone came to follow Christ.[5] These stories are important. However, our conversion story is not our only testimony. Other things have happened since we came to believe in God and came close to Christ. Everyone has faced challenges, doubt, social pressure, testing, failure, alienation from God, etc. One of the most potent testimonies any Christian can give to another person is to tell a story of a struggle in your life similar to a struggle they are having. Once again, people like to hear stories of what God has been doing in the lives of other people they know are Christians. People especially enjoy learning that their Christian friends struggle with the same things they struggle with. Once again, these stories do not have to be dramatic. Sometimes they are more potent if they are not dramatic.

Suppose you were let go from a job, and it took a long time to find a new one. Suppose you prayed, reached out to other Christians, and went to a Christian ministry that helps people find new jobs. Then, after several months of looking, you found a new job! That testimony would mean a lot to someone just laid off from their job. Suppose you have struggled in your marriage, parenting, or some other area of your life, and you prayed that you sensed God's presence in solving the problem. That testimony would be powerful to someone who is experiencing a similar struggle.

We might call these "Continuing Testimonies." God continues to work in our lives after becoming Christians, forming us into the people God wants us to be. This forming process, both pleasant and unpleasant, is part of our continuing testimony. It is also an important witness to what God can do in the life of ordinary people like us.

My former church had a ministry for people looking for a job. It began during a recession, and many people who attended had been let go by their employers in late middle age and had difficulty finding a job. Most sessions began with someone sharing their experience and how God solved the problem. People who found jobs were encouraged to return and tell the newer participants how God had worked in their struggle to find employment. These stories were always crucial to more recent members of the group. People are always encouraged when they can identify with someone who has struggled as they have struggles and come out on the other side.

Appropriate Sharing in Testimonies

One important thing to remember about sharing your testimony is maintaining an appropriate level of self-disclosure. For many years, my wife and I were leaders in the ministry in which laypeople were asked to give their testimonies to others over a weekend. Occasionally, someone would go into great detail about sexual, alcohol, drug, or other indiscretions. These were never good testimonies.

There are two problems with being too explicit: First, as I point out in training sessions, whatever you say to a hundred people is likely to be retold to a more significant number of people. Therefore, it's always a good idea to remember to share at an appropriate level of detail not to embarrass your family, spouse, children, co-workers, or others. Of course, if you were guilty of some sin, it is entirely inappropriate to share the name of someone who may have been involved with you at the time without their express permission.

Second, an explicit repetition of indiscretions borders on glorifying that indiscretion. For example, I once heard a testimony with repeated detailed references to sexual indiscretions. At some point, it almost sounded like bragging. This testimony was given at a retreat where many young men were present. The impression was that this behavior was something that young people do that is fun and exciting but limited and, in the end, disappointing. The testimony almost encouraged the conduct in question. Unfortunately, several young ladies were likely to be hurt by young men who engaged in that pattern of behavior. I felt that this testimony made the wrong point, despite the good intentions of the person who gave it.

It is important to remember that our testimony should not glorify us or our activities, good or bad. A good testimony glorifies God. The level of detail we need to share is that level that allows a listener to understand what God has done in our lives and how important it is to us that God acted to heal us. The point is that God loved and rescued us from the situation—and can be trusted to love and save others. God should be the hero of our testimony, not us.

Ready and Willing to Share our Faith

Many Christians have difficulty sharing their own story. Even more, people are not sure they can tell another person what it means to be a Christian, which is nothing new. Christians have always struggled to share God's love in Jesus Christ with others. The best antidote to our fears is to learn to share a short testimony concerning what God has done in our lives.

Every Christian should be able to give their testimony when appropriate. An excellent way to start is to learn to tell your conversion or another story in about three minutes. If you write it out, that would be about one typed page, double-spaced. Your testimony needs to be personal. It needs to be your story. Of course, it needs to be factually correct. There is a reason why it needs to be short: You may not have a long time to tell it.

I often call this testimony my "Starbucks Testimony." The setting is this: you're at a coffee shop, restaurant, or another place with a friend. During the conversation, it has become appropriate for you to share how you became a Christian. You don't have your Bible. You don't have notes. You don't have your diary. You don't have much time. You're sitting at a table looking at another person. What would you say? What we say will vary from person to person and from situation to situation. What we need to keep in mind is the central point of what we intend to say.

In my particular case, it goes something like this:

> *I grew up in a Christian home. Our family went to church regularly. When I was in college, I drifted away from God. I became selfish and self-centered. I made unwise decisions. Over the next seven years, while I was objectively successful in many people's minds, my life was a mess. In a moment of personal suffering and tragedy, a friend brought me to a Bible study, and that Bible study witnessed to Christ by word and deed. I made Christian friends who shared God's word and love with me. About six months after I was first invited to the Bible study, one afternoon after church, I pondered the worship service and suddenly believed that the Bible was true and that Christ was the Way, the Truth, and the Life. After that moment, my values, objectives, and goals began to change. Over time, some of my worst habits were overcome. God has made a big difference in my life personally, professionally, morally, and spiritually. I've become much different than I was on that day more than forty years ago when I became a Christian.*

After forty years as a Christian leader, I've testified in many different venues, sometimes for as long as two hours. Obviously, in two hours, you share a lot more detail. In one minute, you share a lot less detail. The important thing is to outline in your mind the contours of how you came to Christ so that you can tell the story to another person. Of course, the truths of the Scripture and faith in Christ are primary in the Christian life. However, people are touched by the stories of people whom God has touched. We don't need to worry about having much scripture in our testimony.

Don't Deprive Others of Your Witness

When Christians fail to share what God has done for us with others, we deprive other people of the opportunity to understand what a difference faith in Christ can make in life. A person struggling in their career is touched by the story of a friend who struggled in their career. A person struggling in their marriage is touched by the story of a person who has struggled in marriage. A person struggling with their children is touched by the story of a person struggling with children. Our human stories concerning what God has done in our lives are a source of hope in the lives of others. We must remember this when we are shy or fearful about sharing with others.

We must be able not just to communicate what the Gospel is but also what the Gospel does. A personal testimony should allow another person to see what God has done in the past (the Gospel) and what God continues to do (our testimony). This is why we must continuously be aware of what God is doing and share it. That testimony will touch someone.

In Acts 3, there is a beautiful story about healing involving Peter and John. One day, Peter and John were going to the Temple to pray. As they came to the Temple Gate, there was a lame man. When the man saw Peter and John, he asked for money. Peter, under the inspiration of the Holy Spirit, looked at the man and said, "Silver and gold have I none, but what I do have I give to you: In the name of Jesus Christ of Nazareth, rise and walk" (Luke 3:6). Then, he took a man by the hand and lifted him, and the man was healed. The story ends like this:

> He jumped to his feet and began to walk. Then he went with them
> into the temple courts, walking and leaping and praising God.
> When all the people saw him walking and praising God, they
> recognized him as the same man who used to sit begging at the
> temple gate called Beautiful, and they were filled with wonder and
> amazement at what had happened to him.
>
> (Luke 3:8-10).

The result of this man's willingness to respond to God's healing by walking, jumping, and praising God was that not only did he receive a blessing, but everyone who knew him received a blessing and a sign that God was present. If we keep our Christian faith and what God has done for us a secret, we've been blessed, but the world has not. If we are willing to share all that God is done, we are blessed, and the world is blessed.

We should never be afraid to share what God has done for us. We should never be afraid to "walk and leap and praise God" for the salvation God has given us (Acts 3:6). In Memphis, our church was part of a ministry that sponsored a three-day retreat designed to deepen Christian faith and leadership. As a part of the weekend, I had the opportunity to hear many testimonies. The Biblical content of the weekend talks was outlined for us. We had to say what was supposed to be noted in the talk. On the other hand, we were asked to share a portion of our testimony as a part of our talk.

I have prepared about two dozen teams for the weekends and have listened to the talks during the training sessions. I've heard hundreds of talks during the weekends. Despite all this, I don't remember the exact Biblical or theological content of most of them. I do, however, remember almost every personal testimony. I remember every story of salvation. I remember every marriage that was healed, every addict who recovered from addiction, every criminal who went straight, every homemaker who prayed for a child, every man who ever prayed for a spouse.

Testimonies are important. When we tell others about our faith, we do a fantastic and life-transforming thing. Testimonies of what God has done in our lives reveal to a skeptical world that Christian faith is more than words. God is more than just a distant principal or power who created the heavens and the earth. Instead, God is an active participant in his creation and the lives of his people. He is constantly working to bring love and more wisdom into his people's lives and the universe he created.

Recently, I retired. In the beginning, I was not comfortable with the situation. Then, God opened a door for me to use my gifts in a new church, far away from any congregation I previously served. It was a wonderful experience. This particular testimony resonates with many retired or semi-retired people who need to continue to use their gifts and abilities for the glory of God. Who knows? Perhaps tomorrow, God will give me yet another testimony. The continuing story of what God is doing in our lives is part of what God is doing and about to do in every life we touch. Each day we are alive involves a new act of God that can benefit someone.

Hidden for All the World to See

Some people think that faith should be a private thing. There is a sense in which that is true. One step on the road to hypocrisy is making our faith too much a public matter so that we feel we must continually be seen as religious. No one likes a religious show-off. On the other hand, no one will ever be moved to enter God's family unless they see faith lived out and hear the Gospel in some way. Perhaps the best way to think of how we might present the Gospel is to make our faith "hidden for all the world to see."

We have already talked about the importance of testifying to what God has done in our lives. In addition to a faith hidden for all the world to see, we need to have a publicly proclaimed faith for all the world to hear. There is something about hearing the testimony of someone touched by God that can change everyone who hears that testimony. Speaking out into the world about what God has done for us is integral to being a disciple. However, that verbal testimony must be confirmed and strengthened by what the world sees in the day-to-day lives of Christians.

CHAPTER 9

SHARING IN DIALOGUE

Communicating The Gospel in a New Era

We now come to a central point of this work regarding disciple-making in the emerging postmodern world. Part of the postmodern movement involves changing how people think, moving from an objective idea of truth, in which the observer is an uninvolved reporter, to a relational definition of truth in which understanding is created through a relationship between the observer and reality. [1] In this way of thinking, neither an observer nor an aspect of reality can be separated from the relationship they have with one another. This view is no less rational than the subject-object focus of the modern world. It is just different and requires a different approach to evangelism and discipleship.

Recent cultural developments encourage personal relationships, conversation, and dialogue in disciple-making. It moves Christian disciple-makers away from a "proclamation-centered" view of sharing the Gospel to a relational approach to evangelism. This change is consistent with the Biblical view that faith and understanding flow from a personal relationship between a relational, Triune God and the human race established by grace through God's Word by the Spirit. I believe that the emergence of this way of thinking is a positive development for Christian witness.

Communicating and Community

The word "communicate" has the same root as the words "community" and "communion." We often think of communication as something spoken or transmitted by words or symbols. This way of thinking reduces communication to the transmission of information, leading to the possibility of sharing an impersonal and unbiblical gospel. Authentic communication is not just about *information*; it is about establishing *communion* with another person while seeking to answer the most profound questions of their heart, spoken or unspoken. It means entering into the thought world and emotions of another person in love to establish a deep, trusting, empathetic relationship.

Jesus, when he was with his disciples, was in an intense, personal community with them. He lived, ate, and drank with them. He shared his life with them. The band of followers was a kind of family in which the first disciples received information and, more personally, support, love, advice, and even the physical necessities of life. In this community, the gospel was lived out and shared. When Jesus corrected his disciples, they knew he did so from love and friendship and for no other reason. Often, he knew what they wanted to know even before they asked (See Matthew 12:25; Mark 2:8; Luke 6:8; 11:17). The communication came as a natural result of a life lived in community, conversation and communication.

People See what you Do as well as Hear What You Say.

In child-raising, there is a saying that our children "imitate what we do, not do what we say." Every parent knows this is true. As the disciples spread the gospel, they did not only repeat the information Jesus communicated. They lived out the way of life Jesus lived. Jesus had established a community, and so did the disciples. Here is the way Paul describes it in one of his letters:

> You know how I lived among you the whole time from the first day that I set foot in Asia, serving the Lord with all humility and with tears and with trials that happened to me through the plots of the Jews; how I did not shrink from declaring to you anything that was profitable and teaching you in public and from house to house, testifying both to Jews and to Greeks of repentance toward God and of faith in our Lord Jesus Christ. And now, behold, I am going to Jerusalem, constrained by the Spirit, not knowing what will happen to me there, except that the Holy Spirit testifies to me in every city that imprisonment and afflictions await me. But I do not account my life of any value nor as precious to myself, if only I may finish my course and the ministry that I received from the Lord Jesus to testify to the Gospel of the grace of God.
>
> (Acts 22:18-24)

The Ephesians and others with whom Paul lived and ministered knew who Paul was and how Paul reacted to stress, conflict, opposition, threats, and the like—not just from his words but from his actions and behavior. In times of conflict, Paul could write with authority to those who had lived close to him and knew his heart for God and people (See 2 Corinthians 6:3-13). Paul's effectiveness as a disciple-maker reflected his efficacy as an authentic Christian community builder. Wherever the apostle went, he created and participated in little

Christian communities where he changed people and lives in relationship with Christ, himself, and one another.

Postmodern Communication

The modern world was inclined to see knowledge and information as paramount and relationships as something good, but basically, an "add-on" to the information conveyed or as a technique desirable for better communication of facts. Increasingly, postmodern disciple-making based upon this type of approach is ineffective. From the insights of contemporary physics to communication theory, relationships are paramount. This does not mean Christians do not believe that Jesus is the "Way, the Truth, and the Life." It does not mean that the content of our communication is unimportant. It means that we need to develop ways of communicating such information in the context of human relationships.

As mentioned earlier, postmodern people tend to be profoundly pragmatic and relational. Like our children, they watch to see what difference faith makes in life before committing themselves to any belief system, including Christianity. In such a cultural environment, creating relationships in which people can see faith at work in the lives of others is as important as a verbal message. People want to see the difference Christianity makes. This does not mean that the spoken message is not essential. It just means the relationship may be more critical and longer-lasting in its impact.

Just after the Second World War, the Christian apologist Francis Schaeffer moved to his family in Switzerland and created a community known as L'Abri. Over the years, many people came to L'Abri and participated in the community. Many came to Christ and became Christian leaders. Scholars have critiqued some of the things Schaeffer taught. However, denying the reality and importance of L'Abri as a healing community is impossible.[2] Francis Schaeffer was important in my early Christian walk as both a writer and an example. Today, while I do not agree with some of his ideas, his example of relational discipleship continues to be important to me and all Christians.

Conversations and Dialogue

Contemporary disciple-making can profit from looking at the meaning of both "conversation" and "dialogue." The definition of these terms illuminates the difference between the idea of truth as the result of critical analysis and a relational model of truth. The word "conversation" comes from the Latin root "con" or "with" in English and "vertere," which means "turn" or "bend." Interestingly, like the Hebrew word for knowledge, this particular word was used in the 1500s as a synonym for sexual intercourse and also had a connotation of a household, a manner of conduct and behavior, or a way of life in a home. *In other words, a conversation is an intimate, profoundly human relational activity.*

A conversation is implicitly communal and intended to create communion. It involves a relationship in which two or more individuals share their thoughts and lives in such a way that an understanding that is cognitive, emotional, and spiritual results. Hopefully, their ideas, thoughts, and commitments will be "bent" toward each other in the conversation.

The word "dialogue" has a similar derivation. The Greek roots of this term are "dia," meaning "through," and "logos," meaning "reason." Authentic dialogue happens when two or more persons share meaning by exchanging views. A new understanding emerges as meaning is exchanged and differing points of view illuminate reality.[3] When two or more people enter a dialogue, they commit to a mutual exchange of ideas and information to better understand some aspect of reality. Such a dialogue implicitly seeks a truth that the parties are humble enough to know requires sharing ideas, thoughts, and perspectives.

Humans have dialogues within themselves as they conduct internal conversations about a decision or problem. People also dialogue with another person about a personal business situation. And, of course, we dialogue in a larger context where many people participate. The critical element is the commitment to a relationship of shared wisdom in the context of mutual respect and self-giving love because it accepts uncertainty and difference in the search for authentic community and insight about a situation.

Not so long ago, faced with many difficult decisions in a relatively short time and an organization's future at stake, I often disappeared for a long walk to clear my head. While gone, I would have an internal conversation about a problem. The organization's executive director and I would frequently meet to discuss the issue. We would share our thoughts and opinions about what others suggested we do. In the end, though I was the decision-maker, more often than not, we took her advice because of her superior knowledge of the organization or as a result of the emergence of some third idea that neither of us had previously considered. The benefits of dialogue blessed both of us and the organization.

It is easy to see that if God exists as a community, and if that divine community is a community of shared meaning and love, then some form of conversation or dialogue in which two people can share deep meaning and purpose is most likely the best possible way to share the Gospel. We've already established that God exists in relationship and wants to draw us into relationships of self-giving love of the kind that characterizes the Triune God. That relationship of love cannot be achieved or sustained without deep and personal sharing, which is why conversation and dialogue are a big part of sharing the Christian faith.

In a conversation, we speak what we believe, others share what they think, ask questions to clarify understanding, and modify what we have said to reach a common agreement. Conversing with another person involves sharing a common spiritual, emotional, and intellectual space to share concerns and information deeply. For Christians, this is more important than it would be for non-Christians because of our conviction that the ultimate rationality (the Logos of God) is revealed in the self-giving love Christ showed on the Cross—a passion God shares directly by the Spirit and through believers in Christ.

The Difference between Dialogue and Discussion

Dialogue is different from discussion. Interestingly, the term "discussion" has the same grammatical root as the word "percussion." A discussion can be no more than two people or groups expressing their views, each trying to forcefully convince the other that theirs is the correct view.[4] No real community results. There is only an attempt to persuade or intellectually force agreement. This activity is subject to the postmodern critique that all truth claims are bids for power. Dialogue should not degenerate into mere discussion. Dialogue involves sharing meaning. There must always be an open willingness to hear the other person's views.

Although some proponents of dialogue suggest that we must suspend, give up, or hold in abeyance our views to enter a dialogue, the kind of discussion needed in faith conversations requires that we continue to maintain our beliefs but remember that others do not share these beliefs. We may not be entirely correct in what we think.[5] Therefore, we must learn to be open-minded in sharing the Gospel and what we say. We do not need to give up who we are or what we believe. That would not be authentic. We do not need to agree with everything said by others. We should not do anything like the preceding! We must share our perception of the truth with love and openness to others' opinions and views.

In his book, *Truth to Tell, The Gospel as Public Truth*, Lesslie Newbigin distinguishes between "Agnostic Pluralism" and "Committed Pluralism."[6] Agnostic Pluralism is the kind of pluralism characteristic of our society which assumes that truth is unknowable. There are no criteria for judging between different views. Committed Pluralism sees human beings as capable of actual knowledge of God, subject to human limitations and revision based on new information. In the emerging postmodern reality Christians face today, a Committed Pluralism is needed in which people reach out to others in the Spirit of acceptance and dialogue, communicating their faith in humble, truth-seeking conversations.

The Value of Unintentional Disciple-Making

Many people think evangelism involves only intentional attempts to persuade others of the truth of the Gospel. Some faith conversations occur intentionally, but many discussions arise spontaneously in everyday life. We have conversations with our parents, children, grandchildren, neighbors, business associates, church members, political representatives, people in clubs we belong to, and many others. Only a very few of those conversations begin with a religious premise.

Most conversations are not about a single subject. For example, when our family meets around the dining room table on holidays, we may talk about books for reading, children and grandchildren, politics, the economy, hobbies, church, travel, and many other subjects. No one is in charge of the conversation. It may begin with one person talking about one topic and end with someone else suggesting we change the subject. In between, the conversation moves along a path often subconsciously and generally informally chosen by those involved. [7]

Jesus and Dialogue

When Nicodemus met with Jesus to ask him questions in the middle of the night, the Gospel of John records a long conversation designed to help Nicodemus understand who Jesus is and what Jesus came to do (John 3:1-21). In the next chapter, Jesus meets a nonbeliever at a well in Samaria (John 4). The scene is something like this: Jesus and the disciples are traveling back to Galilee through Samaria. When they reach the town of Sychar, everyone is hungry. Outside of town, there was a well where they chose to stop. (You can see the well today.) The disciples left Jesus at the well and went to town for food.

As Jesus sat by the well resting, a woman came to draw water at an unusual hour. Jesus began the conversation with the woman by asking for a drink from the well since she had brought her bucket to draw water. The woman was surprised that Jesus spoke to her because she was a woman, sexually immoral, and a Samaritan. In Jesus' day, a rabbi was not supposed to speak to women, immoral women, or Samaritan women.

Jesus, ignoring the religious, sexual, and racial conventions of his day, began a conversation with the woman. Initially, the woman misunderstood and spoke of physical water when Jesus spoke of spiritual water. Eventually, Jesus explained to the woman that he is the source of water that permanently quenches a deep human thirst. The woman, who, like most Middle Eastern women of the day, spent a lot of her time gathering water, wanted this kind of water.

This response allowed Jesus to speak into the spiritual life of the woman. Jesus explained that those who drink only physical water and meet physical needs will always be thirsty again. In the spiritual world, those who drink of the love of God will never thirst because they are filled with the source of love. (It has not yet been revealed, but this information meets this woman at the precise point of her need for authentic love.)

The woman then asked for the water. Knowing the woman was not married but living with a man, Jesus asked her to bring her husband to see him. This allowed Jesus to speak into the woman's spiritual and moral condition. Ultimately, the woman understood that God could meet her desire for love without an endless series of men. Once filled with shame and guilt, she experienced the gracious love of God. She then went and told everyone she knew about her conversation with Jesus. As a result, the woman and many other Samaritans become Christ-Followers.

This story helps in understanding the importance of dialogue and conversation. When the woman came to the well, she was an outcast in her society, known to be promiscuous, isolated, and alone. Jesus did not merely proclaim that she was a sinner who could receive restoration by confessing her sins and accepting Him as the Messiah. Instead, he stepped out of Jewish social conventions and formed a relationship with her through a conversation. In the process, the woman received a message about living water and experienced the personal presence of that living water! Jesus healed her relational isolation through a life-transforming conversation.

Jesus did not change the truth he already knew about the woman or her moral and spiritual condition. He knew very well the woman's condition, moral and spiritual. Nevertheless, he did not argue, browbeat, condemn, or judge the woman. He entered into a relationship with her through dialogue—a dialogue in which the woman discovers who Jesus is and that he can heal her relationships.

How this Works out in the Life of a Disciple-maker

Some time ago, my wife and I led a class designed to help people learn to share their faith. One project was learning to share Bible stories from memory. In the second week or so, we learned the story of the woman at the well. In that class, a woman decided she wanted to drop out of the course. Some weeks later, she came back to tell us a story. Not long after dropping out, she had coffee with a friend with marital problems. Infidelity was involved. Her friend was alienated from the Christian faith due to early life experiences.

The friend felt that her husband would never forgive her for what had happened. Our friend casually shared what she remembered about the story of the woman at the well. The other woman, who felt her Christian friends would condemn her, had never heard the story. She left their coffee feeling supported, understood, and loved. I have no idea whether this person became a Christian or not. What is essential is that a Christian shared the love of God with a friend at a critical time in her life. Through a story shared by a Christian friend, the woman felt God's love.

This incident contains important elements to ponder. Our friend was not motivated by the desire to win another soul for God. She was having coffee with an old friend who needed love and support. Although she shared God's love, her purpose was to support and care for another human being. Our friend did not set out to make a gospel presentation or imply that coming to Christ would save her marriage. She just told a story about another woman's situation and allowed her friend to decide how to apply it to her life. Our friend did not demand a commitment or response. She shared the love of Christ with someone in need, communicating care and concern for her friend. [8]

In business, I've had important conversations that involved the Christian faith. However, almost all the time, they were in the context of some legal or business discussion. Years ago, I spent much time with a local investment group manager trying to acquire a company in another state. We had to travel to and from another city and engage in incredibly tedious negotiations with a business owner whose personality and business morals made reaching a deal extremely difficult.

One night while flying home, the manager expressed an interest in my handling of a situation during the negotiations that afternoon. He knew I was a Christian and assumed that my faith had guided my words and actions in the negotiations. He was correct. We then discussed the importance and difficulty of bringing the Christian faith into business dealings. The context of our relationship was not religious, nor was the situation a ministerial meeting. It was a business negotiation.

Nevertheless, both of us grew in our faith due to our conversation on the airplane. I learned from him, and he learned from me. It was a dialogue before I knew what dialogue was. Incidentally, we were ultimately successful in acquiring the business.

Dialogue in a Lonely, Isolated Society

In a society characterized by loneliness and isolation, in which many people feel unloved and alone, caring relationships in which the Gospel is communicated with compassion are vital. The fundamental prerequisite is to be centered in love for others, not driven by any agenda, including the Gospel. The most important thing we do is empathetically love the other person.

Of course, a few valuable techniques help center a conversation on the needs of the other.

First, there is a technique known as "reflective listening." Reflective listening involves responding to the other by rephrasing what they have said to be sure you understand what they are saying. A lot of the time, we think we know what another person is saying, but we do not. We have misunderstood. Learning to listen and pay close attention to what another person is saying is essential.

Second, we must be aware of our emotional responses. People can often say things that are either shocking or opposed to what we deeply believe. In such situations, we cannot help but be emotionally impacted. As a pastor, I have had many such experiences. Much of the time, if we are not self-aware, we end up responding too quickly and often too strongly. Our "body language" almost certainly communicates our shock. When we experience such an emotional response, it is best to remain silent until we can respond in the kindest possible way. [9]

For example, I tend to look away from a person if I genuinely disagree with what they are saying. When I look away, I am listening, but the other person senses a disconnect. Looking away often involves formulating a response to what is being said before the person is finished speaking. Although the other person may not know I am developing a reply (which they would not appreciate), they usually know I am not paying attention to what they are saying! The best practice is to pay close physical and mental attention to the other person until they have finished speaking.

The Fruit of Dialogue

It is impossible to overestimate the fruitfulness of learning to have loving conversations with others personally, professionally, and spiritually. In particular, learning to have a good conversation is an essential element in being a good disciple-maker. Of course, dialogue is vital as a person asks questions and explores what it would mean to become a disciple of Jesus. It is crucial to have answers to some questions. Knowing a gospel presentation and having a personal testimony is essential. But the most important thing is to be in a loving conversation with another person.

The conversations and dialogues we have with people after they have become Christ-Followers are just as important as those we have before they follow Jesus. People do not become perfect disciples the moment they accept Christ. Like us, people resist change, make mistakes, hide their faults and shortcomings, and fear rejection if they are honest about their struggles. To help people at critical junctures in their walk with Christ, we must remain open, non-judgmental, diplomatic, and conversational as we help them "learn to obey all Christ has commanded."

As mentioned at the beginning, our business as disciple-makers involves more than getting people to the point that they accept Christ as their Lord and Savior. Our business as disciple-makers is to help them become deeply committed, mature disciples of Christ. The ability to walk and share with others, learn and grow together as both the disciple-maker and disciple to lovingly grow together in Christ is not easy, but it is the most rewarding thing we can do to show God's love to those around us.

CHAPTER 10

DISCIPLES HAVE A WAY OF LIFE

B eing a disciple of Jesus involves more than recognizing who Jesus is. Discipleship consists of trusting God while living the kind of life Jesus lived. The Great Commission asks disciples to do more than witness to new believers. It asks Christians to teach new believers "to obey all that I have commanded you" (Matt. 28:20). This task includes teaching disciples the fundamentals of a new way of life by word and example (I Peter 5:3). Words are not enough. Faithful and obedient wisdom and a life of self-giving love are the goals of Christian discipleship.

In Second Corinthians, Paul says that if anyone comes to Christ, they are a new "creation" (2 Corinthians 5:17). In other words, new disciples are new newborn babies in Christ. This means that helping people come to Christ is not enough. Just like children, new disciples need to be taught what the new life in Christ is like! Just as children need parents, new disciples need examples, and teachers, mentors in Christ.

A Tradition of Wisdom and Love

Much contemporary teaching about evangelism and discipleship implies that to be a good disciple of Christ, a person needs to be "radical." This approach is attractive in a culture that encourages extreme individualism. A negative aspect of this approach is that it implies that ordinary people with conventional lives and pre-existing responsibilities must completely alter their lives and radically change their lives to be real disciple-making followers of Christ. This notion is both true and untrue. New believers do need a radical transformation—but the nature of that transformation is spiritual and not necessarily visible all the time. The changes in how we think, feel, and respond to life may or may not always be seen by others.

In his work, *Fear and Trembling,* Soren Kierkegaard describes the "Knight of Faith" as potentially an ordinary person who goes about his daily life with nothing about his exterior that would clue an observer to the fact that this person was indeed extraordinary "solid through and through":

This man takes pleasure, takes part, in everything and whenever one catches him occupied with something his engagement has the persistence of the worldly person whose soul is wrapped up in such things. He minds his affairs. [2]

The true disciple of Christ is distinguished by the love and wisdom with which they live their day-to-day life, not by their radical difference from those around them. Of course, as time goes by, hopefully, people see a radical difference—a radical difference in love, care for others, willingness to suffer for the world, and wisdom that is deeper than mere shrewdness and self-interest. However, few people may be able to discern the difference.

Disciples are called to live wisely, love others unconditionally, and imitate Jesus Christ. As we follow Jesus, our lives change, but that may or may not mean changing our careers, friendships, lifestyle, location, etc. After becoming Christians, many people continue to live where they formerly lived, in the profession and occupation they previously had, now sharing God's wisdom and love with their family, neighborhood, community, friends, and fellow workers in a new way. This was true in the early church as well as today. Not everyone was a Peter or Paul.

The contemporary "radical" ideal of Christianity is an import from an Enlightenment mentality with its reflexive idea that what previously existed (tradition) is corrupt and backward. [3] In this way of thinking, what is to come (revolutionary change) is better than what is now. From the French Revolution forward, this way of thought has led to disaster after disaster. A radical personality can lead to all kinds of social and personal suffering.

Instead of the modern toxic glorification of continual and often mindless change, Christians are called to exhibit wise and loving personal and communal order. Some things need to change and will change due to a new life in Christ, but not everything. What does need to change is anything that prevents us from living wisely with self-giving love toward God and others. What needs to be preserved are those historical patterns of wise and wholesome living that created the civilization we enjoy. Christians can and must adapt to the future, but not at the expense of wisdom and love for people.

People of the Way

The earliest name for Christians was "People of the Way" (Acts 9:2). The first Christians, most of whom lived lives structured by the Law of Moses and Jewish customs, found in Christ a new way to God through faith in Christ. This new way did not involve following a lot of external rules by exercising human willpower. It involved living on the basis of faith in the forgiveness, love, and new life offered by Christ.

This new approach did not mean the moral law was eliminated (Romans 6). Jesus specifically taught that he came not to abolish the law but to complete it (Matthew 5:17). The completion involves a relationship with God in Christ, a relationship through which disciples are filled with the Holy Spirit and empowered to live in wise, wholesome, loving relationships with God, other people, and creation (Romans 8).

The writer of Daniel promises faithful Jews that they will shine like stars with the wisdom of God (Daniel 12:3). Jesus urged his believers to live lives that shine with the love of God and others (Matthew 5:16). Paul urges believers to live in such a way that the disciples "shine like stars" amid first century Greco-Roman culture (Philippians 2:15). This promise is for every generation of believers. As people of the Way, the ordinary, day-to-day lives of disciples should shine into the lives of others with the power of God's Spirit of wisdom and love.

The earliest Christians saw in Jesus a way to experience forgiveness of sins and a new mode of living in relationship and harmony with God and others. Jesus summarized this manner of life as loving God and others. When asked which was the greatest of the commandments, Jesus replied:

> Love the Lord your God with all your heart and with all your soul and with all your mind. This is the first and greatest commandment. And the second is like it: Love your neighbor as yourself.
> (Matthew 22:37-39)

Living out the love of God in our day-to-day lives is the primary duty of a Christian. Everything else flows from this first decision for unselfish, self-giving love.

Salt and Light

In the Sermon on the Mount, Jesus has these words for his disciples:

> You are the salt of the earth. But how can the salt be made salty again if it loses its saltiness? It is no longer good for anything except to be thrown out and trampled underfoot. You are the light of the world. A town built on a hill cannot be hidden. Neither do

people light a lamp and put it under a bowl. Instead, they put it on its stand, and it gives light to everyone in the house. In the same way, let your light shine before others, that they may see your good deeds and glorify your Father in heaven.

(Matthew 5:13-16)

These words remind us that it is not just what we say that matters. It is what we are that matters. We are to be salt and light. We are to shine with the light of Christ. In shining with the light of Christ, we are to preserve and give health to the world around us.

Salt is a physical mineral. Light illuminates the world and allows us to see where we are going. Salt gives flavor and is a healing agent. Light is an antiseptic and healing agent and a source of illumination. Jesus described himself as "The Light of the World", saying, "I am the light of the world. Whoever follows me will never walk in darkness, but will have the light of life" (John 8:12). To be a disciple is both to walk in the light that is Christ and to reflect that light into the world (Matthew 5:14).

Jesus wants us to live in such a way that we are a preservative and healer of the foolishness and brokenness of the world. He wants us to have wisdom in how we love others so that we become a light that shines into the darkness (Philippians 2:15). The light of God shining in our lives can and should attract people. This is not so radical as it is entirely unexpected but fundamentally the wisest and best way to live.

A Matter of Grace

All this sounds legalistic until we remind ourselves that we are saved by grace. God's grace empowers disciples to live the Christian life (Ephesians 2:8-9). By his mercy, God calls us into a relationship with Christ, and we cannot live the Christian life without the presence and power of God sustaining our spiritual life. The first step towards hypocrisy is to forget the central importance of grace, God's mercy, and the gift of the Spirit in our daily Christian life. When we forget our dependence on God's grace, sooner or later, we lose that intimate fellowship with God that allows us to walk in the Way of Christ and share that way with others.

When we allow God to illuminate and empower us by the Holy Spirit, we reflect the power of God in our day-to-day lives. Of course, we fail and fall short—more often than we would like. Nevertheless, if we remain in Christ, and continue to live based on grace, asking God to enter our lives and transform us, we progress.

When teaching about the life of grace, I like to say, "I am not the person I ought to be, but thank God I am also not the person I used to be! We are not the people we were yesterday, last week, last month, or last year if we allow God's grace to transform our lives. We make progress because the Spirit of God is working in us.

Means of Grace for the New Way

Theologians have ways of talking about how God allows us to grow in Christ. The term "Means of Grace" describes how God works in our lives so that we grow in Christ. These means of grace are essential because they are how we remain connected to the source of our new life in Christ. Of course, the primary means by which we become and grow as a disciple is in a relationship with the risen Christ. Jesus called disciples into a personal relationship, and Christians ever since have called people into a relationship with Jesus. This relationship changes believers from the inside out.

Paul begins his letter to the Colossians by reminding the Colossians who Jesus was. He is the image of God's inhuman form (1:15). Christ is the vehicle through whom the universe and everything in it were made (1:16). Christ is the head of the church, those called out by God to proclaim his glory (1:18). He reconciles creation and people to one another so that God's peace can prevail (1:19-20). He is the source of forgiveness of sins and fellowship with God the Father (1:21). In Christ, our old life is put to death. We receive a new life (3:1). Christ is the Logos, the Word of God, who embodies the wisdom by whom and through whom every-thing was made (John: 1:3). Christian faith is not irrational or foolish but rational in the deepest possible way—a way the world sometimes thinks is ridiculous.

In response to what God has done, believers live a different life because a different kind of life, God's life, is growing inside us. This putting on of a new life is described both as a dying to an older type of life, characterized by passions, immorality, evil desires, greed, covetousness, malice, slander of others, and ob-scenity and the like, and the growth of a new kind of life characterized by love, joy, peace, patience, kindness, self-control, and the like (Galatians 5:17-21).

As we overcome our personalities' dark, sinful side, we begin to experience a new kind of life. Here is how Paul describes this new life:

> Therefore, as God's chosen people, holy and dearly loved, clothe
> yourselves with compassion, kindness, humility, gentleness, and
> patience. Bear with each other and forgive one another if any of
> you has a grievance against someone. Forgive as the Lord forgave

you. And beyond these virtues, put on love, which binds them
all together in perfect unity. Let the peace of Christ rule in your
hearts, since, as members of one body, you were called to peace.
And be thankful. Let the message of Christ dwell among you richly
as you teach and admonish one another with all wisdom through
psalms, hymns, and songs from the Spirit, singing to God with
gratitude in your hearts. And whatever you do, whether in word or
deed, do it all in the name of the Lord Jesus, giving thanks to God
the Father through him.

(Colossians 3:12-17)

Notice that it is not primarily *behaviors* that Paul urges on the Colossians but
spiritual qualities people receive as they remain in a relationship with Christ.
Compassion, kindness, humility, gentleness, patience, forgiveness, and love are
spiritual qualities we receive by Grace as we allow Christ to work in our hearts.
Growing in Christ involves behavior; however, most importantly, it consists in
developing new spiritual qualities.

God works through his Word, Christ, and the Holy Spirit's power. God also
works through "Sacraments" or "Sacred Acts." These sacred actions involve
physical elements, bread, wine, water, oil, the laying on of hands, rings, etc.,
which symbolize God's more profound, spiritual action in the life of believers.
These acts are sacred because God is present uniquely in the life of the person
experiencing the sacrament.

Baptism

One of the first things we do when we become Christians and encourage others to do when they become Christ-Followers is experiencing the sacred rite of
baptism as we celebrate new life in Christ and profess our faith to the world.
If we were baptized as children or even earlier in our lives as adults, it may be
necessary to "own" the new life we have received by publicly renewing our baptism.[5] Some groups immerse, some pour the water on a new believer, and some
sprinkle. By whatever means a baptism is accomplished, water is administered,
signifying leaving the old life and beginning a new life in Christ.

In some groups, parents baptize their children when relatively young as a
sign that God is already working his salvation in their lives through his covenant
promises to the child's parents. If a new believer has never been baptized, they
are baptized as a sign of their new faith. Some denominations baptize only adults
on a profession of faith. Even if there has been an infant baptism, in some cases,
a believer will want to renew that Baptism in a Renewal of Baptism service that

is much like a baptism, except that it is a renewal of a prior baptism and not a baptism. [6]

Some years ago, a lady in our congregation married a man who had been in her life some years earlier. She had always remembered and loved him. When he left, he was in a lifestyle that was not, by any definition, Christian. Years later, God brought them back together. This person became a friend, prayer partner, and fellow worker in our congregation and a Christian ministry in our area. One of the great privileges of my life was the day we baptized my friend! We used to see each other almost weekly, and once or twice a year, we would take time to remember that "sacred moment" in his life when he publicly declared his faith in Christ and his commitment to be a disciple of Christ.

Christ-Centered Worship

A disciple is regular in worship. We cannot enter the family life of God, Father, Son, and Holy Spirit, without worshiping in community with others who have responded to God's call to show his light and love in the world. Although the Word is at the center of all Christian worship of whatever kind, it is like a jewel in a precious setting. Calls to worship, songs and hymns, confession, readings from scripture, the people's prayers, the sermon, the Eucharist, or Lord's Supper—all the liturgical aspects of worship deepen our walk with Christ. [7]

There is truth in the saying of St. Cyprian that "One cannot have God as his father and not have the Church as his mother." [8] When I was younger, I went through a period when I did not attend worship and was not part of a Christian community. Not surprisingly, I drifted away from the Christian faith and developed bad habits. This is the inevitable result of cutting oneself off from the people of God.

While Christians believe it is possible to live the Christian life without living within and worshiping as part of the community of faith, ordinarily, this should not happen. Most of us can take time to worship God regularly. We can hear the Word in community with others. We should thank God we can be in community, for there are those who cannot because of age, infirmity, or other necessities.

As Christians grow older, it is not uncommon for them to become homebound. Sometimes, it may be necessary to miss church because of other responsibilities. Recently, many people have been forced to avoid public places. Fortunately, most people can be part of a regular small group, and modern technology has provided means for providing some form of worship for those who cannot attend for health or other reasons.

The Lord's Supper

Once a Christian is part of a church, sooner or later, they participate in a Communion Service. Different groups have different names for such a service. In Catholic Churches, it is called the "Eucharist." Protestant congregations call it the "Lord's Supper" or "Communion." By whatever name it is called, Christians believe faith is strengthened by this service of remembrance and spiritual participation in Christ's sacrificial death on the cross. Most Christians believe God is especially present through the power of the Holy Spirit in a life-changing way when we share the Lord's Supper. [9]

Some groups have a service called a "Love Feast," in which small groups celebrate a meal in which the love of Christ and the unity of the group are celebrated. Love Feasts are not communion services for those groups in which an ordained clergy must be present for the Lord's Supper to be celebrated. Whatever the case, remembering and contemplating the love of God present in Christ strengthens our faith. [10] These love feasts allow smaller groups of Christians to renew and mature in faith for groups with this tradition.

Public and Private Prayer

Because discipleship is a life of relationship with God through Christ by the power of the Holy Spirit, the life of a disciple is strengthened and deepened by prayer. Once again, prayers should and will be said in worship, small groups, and other places where Christians gather. Nevertheless, daily private prayer is a fundamental way Christians grow in discipleship. [11]

At the beginning of the Christian walk, prayers may be selfish and even a bit simple. That is fine. When a small child begins to talk, their conversations are not complicated or profound. As a child grows and matures, their ability to communicate grows and deepens. This is true in the life of faith. This particular part of the Christian life is of such importance that it is discussed again in more detail in a later chapter. For now, it is vital to encourage the practice of communal and private prayer in the life of every disciple.

For Christians, prayer is not so much a means to an end as a conversation with the Friend of All Friends—God. As we spend time with God, our friendship deepens and grows. Initially, we may ask for things our friend thinks are harmful or destructive. Our friend does not respond. Over time, we learn that fact about our friends. In the beginning, when prayers are not answered, we may think our friend has deserted us. Only much later will we know that our friend is present even in his silence and immovable intention not to answer a particular prayer. In the end, we have something more important than answered prayers. We will have a deep relationship with God.

I have a good friend with whom I often meet for lunch. When we are together, there is no set agenda. We are not at lunch to get something from one another. We are there to be with one another and enjoy the company of one another. Sometimes, we have very little to say to one another. We are just happy to be together. This is what our prayer life should be like.

Confession

There is probably no area of Christian life more neglected by Christians, particularly Protestants, than the regular confession of sins and shortcomings. Confession is that act by which human beings acknowledge to God and to those we have offended the things we have done that ought not to have been done and not done that should have been done. For an authentic Christian community to exist, there must be a willingness to be open about sins and shortcomings and acceptance of the sins and weaknesses of others. Confession is essential for healing guilt and shame and the division that sins, and shortcomings bring in any fellowship.

Interestingly, in *Life Together*, Dietrich Bonhoeffer spends an entire chapter of a five-chapter book on the importance of confession to the Christian life. He begins his analysis by noting that many Christian fellowships have a façade of camaraderie but not the deep fellowship resulting from a shared understanding of sin and human brokenness. This observation is accurate in my experience and the experience of many pastors and church leaders. Too often, our churches and Christian groups become inauthentic groups of outwardly thriving but inwardly dying Christians who cannot or will not open up about the sin in their lives.

In confession, sin is cleansed, and any façade of righteousness that inhibits the growth of true discipleship is broken. In confession, there is a "breakthrough to authentic Christian community." [12] Hypocrisy is overcome by the willingness to see ourselves as broken and sinful creatures needing grace. In addition, in confession, there is a breakthrough to authentic personal Christian life and growth in wisdom and love. Confession opens us up to a new future, free of the impediments that have prevented us from becoming the people God wants us to be.

Confession need not be to a priest or a religious professional. Confession can be made to any mature Christian, though the custom is for the priest or pastor to hear confessions in certain groups. Spiritual directors or "staretz" may hear confessions in the Orthodox Church and other fellowships. In some groups, an emphasis is made on going to the person one has offended. In other groups, this is not necessary. Sometimes, it might be hurtful if the offended knew the offense's details.

In some cases, it may be appropriate to make amends. In every case, it is vital to acknowledge the sin, receive forgiveness, and move forward without relapsing into the behaviors of the past. All this can take time, sometimes a great deal of time.

New Christians will not necessarily know the power of confession nor the continuing work of grace and renewal in the Christian life. Therefore, becoming accustomed to confessing one's faults and receiving forgiveness can be difficult. Through the small fellowship of a group of Christians, all of whom acknowledge their status and are sinners in need of grace, this aspect of the life of discipleship best grows.

Works of Love

Jesus involved his disciples in his work of love to the world. [13] In the Gospels and Acts, the disciples do acts of healing, compassion, and mercy towards others. Although God is interested in our internal spiritual life, humans are physical creatures. Self-giving love, the essential virtue of a Christian, by its nature, must be enacted and lived in our day-to-day lives. Experience teaches that those who never put their faith into practice serving God and others don't grow.

New disciples need to develop the habit of serving others in some way. These acts of service can be both personal, such as giving to the needs of others, individual actions of mercy, visiting the sick, caring for those in need, and the like, and public, such as being involved in solving social problems, overcoming injustices, and the like. As we change our priorities and move out of selfish self-seeking and into loving service to others, we grow in discipleship.

My duties as a pastor often caused me to study a fair bit of the week. I found that if I did not take time to visit the sick, be involved in some ministry outside of our congregation, and serve others, sooner or later, I began to feel dry, and my faith became joyless. The best cure for this problem was and is to get up and do something for someone else. This is true of nearly all Christians. To grow in our faith, we need to put that faith to work in acts of love. In addition, as already emphasized, people, including unbelievers, notice when Christians put their faith to work.

Walking the Walk as well as Talking the Talk

The bottom line is this: if we are to lead other people, and especially new believers, into a deeper walk with Christ, we must be attentive to our discipleship and to ways in which we can draw others more deeply into a life of discipleship. Assuming we regularly attend church, one sure way to help another person internalize the Word and participate in the Sacraments is to invite them to join us at church or a discipleship group. The same is true of Bible studies, prayer groups, and other Christian ministries in which we participate.

Once again, new and old disciples, like children, "catch" more than they are "taught" what it means to be a disciple. Many years ago, as a layperson and an elder in a local congregation, I had the habit of visiting people who were sick in our Sunday school class. I did not always visit, but I did visit a good bit. Over the years, people have mentioned how much that meant to them. Years later, when I was in seminary, one of our members had a severe heart attack. Although I wrote a card, I could not visit. I was heartbroken that I could not visit my friend. Other people in his Sunday school class did visit my friend and his spouse. Others saw what was being done, and I am sure that people visit the sick many years later without being told or asked because they saw it modeled.

My father-in-law was in the food business. After he retired, he developed the habit of going around town to Houston's bakeries and picking up bread and other items. He then distributed them to local ministries. It was his way of actively serving the body of Christ even though he was retired and beyond the time when he could do many things he had always done. We all need to have such ministries of care and compassion.

One good friend was a successful businessperson in a very competitive business. As the leader of his company, he demonstrated the love of Christ in his dealings with others in the industry. Our secular occupations can be our best witness for Christ if we have one. Some time ago, I attended a funeral for a High School coach. I watched as men of all ages went to the podium to testify to the difference this person made in their lives. This person's job as a coach was his mission field.

The Transforming Way

Several times in this and past chapters, we have had the opportunity to describe the Christian life as a Way. This description alerts us to the fact that Christians have distinctive beliefs about God and the world that lead to a distinctive way of life, a way of life that is different. Parts of that Way of life cannot be seen. It is hidden. Prayer is an example. Parts of that way of life are public. Attendance at worship is an example. The transformation we experience in Christ is both public and private. In the end, no part of our existence is untouched by the love and wisdom of God.

PART 3

BEING A DISCIPLE
IN A FRAGMENTED AGE

CHAPTER 11

THE WAY OF PRAYER

Prayer: The Inner Life of a Disciple

Can you imagine walking and living with someone daily and never conversing with them? Can you imagine a family never communicating? A married couple? Partners in a business? Of course not! If discipleship involves a deep, personal, long-term relationship with God in Christ, following Jesus day-by-day and learning from him, then disciples must be able to commune with God through Christ.

Prayer is the vital communication link that permits our relationship with God to grow and deepen. Just as a relationship with a spouse continues to evolve and grow, we never reach the end of growth in our prayer life. Our relationship with God grows, changes, and deepens as our walk with God grows and deepens daily. In this way, our relationship with God is no different than our relationship with any other person: We must take time to be in communion with another person.

When I first became a Christian, I had trouble learning to pray. Over the years, I found that the best way to learn to pray is to pray, learning at each stage of discipleship what you need to move forward in the life of prayer. No one can ever learn all there is to know about communicating with God, just as no person can ever know all there is to know about human communication. What we can know is something we can put into practice today! If we continue to open our lives to the Spirit of God, we will grow in our prayer life.

We live in a post-Christian society. Many people did not grow up in Christian homes, with parents helping them learn to pray. They never attended Sunday School or Vacation Bible School. They never prayed in church with other members of the congregation. They never experienced the prayers of family, friends, or fellow church members. Those who grew up in Christian homes may never have seen or heard their parents and friends pray. Many of these people live in a "soulless world" where there is no room for a God of Love who cares for them and wants to get to know them. They grew up thinking that a material universe is all there is or can be.

For these people, prayer can be a foreign experience. Nevertheless, in times of suffering and pain, most people cry out for help, even from the God they do not know, whose character is written upon their hearts. (In fact, this instinctive human propensity to pray is one reason for believing there is a personal God.) It is not that people cannot pray or the inner inclination to pray. [1] They do. The problem is that they have never developed a personal relationship with God such that they can lift their needs to God in a natural way. Once such people open their hearts to God, their God-given capacity for prayer can be developed and enhanced. Maturity in the life of the Spirit is dependent upon moving from a state of prayer immaturity to prayer maturity.

Even among Christians who know something about prayer, many are reluctant to pray. Prayer is an act of self-revelation. Some people are afraid of what they might say. Others are afraid that they will not be able to pray as well as a professional, such as a pastor or group leader. These fears can deprive a new disciple of a vibrant prayer life. Opening up in honest prayer in front of family, friends, fellow church members, and others can be as embarrassing as being seen without clothes on. Our False Self—our façade of control, of capacity to solve our problems—must come down for us to learn to pray honestly concerning our fears, faults, and failures. [2] There is no hiding who we are in honest prayer.

A Disciple is a Person of Prayer

Like discipleship, prayer is not something we learn **about**; it is something we learn to **do**. Like all skills, no one is accomplished at the beginning of their prayer life. Instead, by trial and error, long experience, praying well and poorly, rightly and wrongly, maturely and immaturely, slowly but surely, a prayer life grows and deepens. This has been my experience and the experience of most Christians. In prayer, like pitching a baseball, you begin learning to throw a simple fastball, and then you improve your game by adding other pitches.

Because prayer is a skill, it is essential to keep practicing and learning. A disciple needs to be a person of prayer, and a disciple of fifty years should be a better person of prayer than a disciple of fifteen minutes—and they will be if they keep praying. A few years ago, I went on an eight-day silent retreat. For a week, about twenty-five of us did nothing but pray silently. We prayed in groups, alone, in journals, on walks, while running, etc. We prayed prayers from Scripture, in writing, and in silent contemplation of God. Once a day, we prayed out loud in worship. Forty years ago, I could not have endured such a long silence and prayer!

Learning to Pray

Most Christians learn to pray by watching someone else pray. People born into Christian homes learn to pray, hearing parents pray at meals or bedtime. Before long, we were saying our prayers just before we went to bed. As we attended Church with our parents, we listened to the pastor pray and prayed from a bulletin or prayer book. In Sunday School, we heard prayers and then learned to pray ourselves. Perhaps we saw our parents praying under challenging circumstances or over difficult decisions. As we matured, we learned to pray under the pressure of difficult times in life.

This description of how people learn to pray alerts us to the need for mature Christians to help new Christians in their discipleship families learn to pray. As necessary as books, tapes, videos, classes, and other learning opportunities to pray are, nothing can replace a personal relationship with someone who models prayer for a new or growing Christian. Prayer involves a personal relationship with God and is best taught within a personal relationship with another person. This can be a family member, a friend, a small group leader, a Sunday School teacher, a pastor, or anyone else who prays regularly.

As a new Christian, I was good at reading my Bible, attending church, and being involved in specific ministries. I was not good at praying. I am naturally an active person. Sitting silently, praying, and listening to God was (and is) hard for me. Therefore, I did what people who like to read do: I bought a book, *Prayer*, by George A. Buttrick. [3] It did not take long to realize that reading a 300-page book would not likely improve my prayer life. Therefore, I took a different tactic. I just started praying.

Then, I found a short prayer guide focused on adoration, confession, thanksgiving, and personal requests (supplication), the so-called "ACTS method" of prayer. I listened to people pray who were in Bible studies I attended. Several years later, I was part of an early morning prayer group that met for a couple of years during a difficult time in an organization we were a part of. This group stretched and improved my prayer life. In seminary, a small group met weekly for prayer and had prayer partners. Once in ministry, I developed habits of prayer that continue to this day. In a challenging period in ministry, I started another prayer discipline: praying the scriptures and a kind of Christian contemplation on Christ. One summer, I went away for an eight-day silent prayer time to deepen my prayer relationship with God. More recently, I began keeping a long prayer list. Sometimes, I write out prayers in my journal. All these disciplines did not come naturally or easily. They just appeared at the right time in my life of discipleship. The same thing is true of nearly all Christians. Disciple-makers must get a person started in the life of prayer.

Jesus and Prayer

Jesus had a simple method for teaching his disciples to pray: he prayed. Jesus prayed at every turning point in his life and ministry. Matthew tells us that, after Jesus fed the 5000, he went out alone and prayed: "After he had dismissed his disciples, he went up on a mountainside by himself to pray" (Matt. 14: 23). At the end of his life, Jesus prayed for release from the momentous task ahead of him. Mark describes it this way: "Going a little farther, he fell to the ground and prayed that if possible, the hour might pass from him. 'Abba, Father,' he said, 'everything is possible for you. Take this cup from me. Yet not what I will, but what you will'" (Mark 14:35-36). From the beginning to the end of his earthly ministry, Jesus was a person of prayer.

His disciples recognized prayer as the secret of Jesus' unusual wisdom, goodness, and power. Therefore, the disciples asked Jesus to teach them to pray (Luke 11:1). In response to their request; he taught them what has always been considered the model prayer. By the time of the Sermon on the Mount, the disciples had been with Jesus for a while. They had seen miracles, healings, exorcisms, and the like. They had heard his teachings and his preaching. They had eaten many meals together. They had experienced his hidden, secret, silent power. They had seen him pray and go away to be alone in prayer. They had noticed that Jesus was a person of prayer, and somehow his prayer life was deeply a part of who he was and his mission and ministry. Therefore, it was natural that they should ask him to teach them to pray.

The Basics

In response, Jesus gave them (and us) a few basic things to remember. He begins with some general instructions:

> **First, our prayers are to be directed to God**. Jesus prayed to
> his Heavenly Father. This does not mean we cannot use differ
> ent words to refer to the One True God, the Father Almighty, the
> Maker of Heaven and Earth. We can pray to God, the Eternal God,
> the Almighty, God the Healer, the Triune God, the One Who Is,
> and the like. We can direct our prayers to Jesus and the Holy Spirit,

but we must remember that we are referring all those prayers to the Triune God whom Jesus called "Father." In particular, we don't pray to other gods, natural forces, new age figures, crystals, or the like, Just the God of Love revealed in Christ.

Second, we should pray from the heart. Jesus tells his disciples to pray in secret (Matthew 6:6). He does so to remind them (and us) not to pray to show off, show how spiritual we are, try to gain the praise of other people, show off our personal prayer language, or for any reason other than to communicate with God. Although we use our minds as we pray, our heart connecting to the heart of God is at stake in prayer. This is why silent and contemplative prayers are still prayers: our human heart connects with God's divine heart.

Third, we should be careful about "babbling" (Matt. 6:7). We should not pray words just to be seen praying words, nor should we think that we will get a better response from God just because we use many words. Christians should pray rationally, that is, reasonably. We should be careful not to pray nonsense or repeat a request 1000 times, hoping to force God's hand. We should not make our prayer life a time of emotional self-exposure, irrational, or showing off. If we are occasionally overcome with emotion, we pray incredibly passionately, that's fine. If we periodically repeat a phrase or a request, that is fine. If we have a deep prayer for a family member or ourselves that we must pray over and over for years, that is fine. Jesus' instructions were not meant to be hard and fast rules but things to do and avoid doing.

The Two Tablets of the Lord's Prayer

Having given some primary teaching on what prayer should be like, Jesus gave his disciples an example in a prayer we all know as the Lord's Prayer.[4] In its historical form, the Lord's Prayer goes like this:

Our Father, which art in heaven,
Hallowed be thy Name. Thy Kingdom come,
Thy will be done. On earth as it is in heaven.
Give us this day our daily bread.
And forgive us our trespasses,
As we forgive those that trespass against us.

And lead us not into temptation, but deliver us from evil.
For thine is the kingdom, the power, and the glory,
For ever and ever.
Amen.[5]

Pastors, scholars, and others have noticed that it is possible to understand the prayer as divided into two halves, much like the Ten Commandments, with one half being about our relationship with God and the other half being about ourselves and our needs.[6] It begins by invoking "Our Father who art in Heaven." This is meant to indicate that we are not praying to a force, to an impersonal deity, but to a person—our Heavenly Father, who loves us and can be trusted to hear our prayers. Because God is personal, we believe he listens and responds to prayers, even if the answer is "no" or "not yet."

When we pray "Hallowed Be Thy Name," we recognize and invoke the God who gave us his Name on Mt. Sinai and who is holy and whom we should recognize as absolutely sacred. This means that God is wholly other, different from us, not under our control, and not subject to our complete scrutiny. In the end, we cannot fully understand God. We can only worship God. God's holiness also means that God is uncontaminated by sin, self-interest at the expense of others, and limitations or flaws. Therefore, God can be trusted to hear and respond to our prayers in love.

Second, we pray for God's Kingdom to come "on earth as it is in Heaven." This is where the Gospel and discipleship begin to enter into our prayers in a meaningful way. When we pray for God's Kingdom to come, we pray that God's mercy, wisdom, justice, peace, and love will come into our broken world. We pray that old divisions be healed, that wars cease, that the poor, widows, and others in need be cared for, that those unjustly imprisoned be released, and that those mistreated be treated fairly. We pray that our world will become like heaven itself. This is when we can speak to God about significant issues, war, peace, government, etc. Jesus came proclaiming the Kingdom of God, and every day we should pray for that kingdom to come to us in some way that day.

Third, having prayed to God for big things, we pray for ourselves. When we pray for our daily bread, we pray for the necessities of life. We pray for the things we need for ourselves, our family, friends, neighbors, and those we love and care about. This prayer brings our faith into our most mundane, everyday needs. We all need clothing, food, shelter, family wholeness, an income, and other things. God wants us to lift these needs to his throne of Grace.

Fourth, we pray to forgive those who have wronged us. If our first prayers are for physical needs, our second prayers are for our moral and emotional needs, our need to be forgiven and forgive others. Jesus warns his disciples that it is not healthy to hold grudges. It is not healthy to live with an unforgiving heart. If we cannot bring ourselves to forgive others, this lack of forgiveness interferes with our prayers for forgiveness (Matt. 7:14-15).

Our personal wholeness is deeply related to achieving relational wholeness with God and others. Just as those who have wronged us need forgiveness, we also need forgiveness. In this regard, God reminds us that if we expect to be forgiven, we had best get about the business of forgiving others. Since we are all flawed in some way and hurt others, forgiving others is a part of our solidarity with the entire human race filled with fallen, imperfect, and finite people just like us.

Finally, we pray to be delivered from evil. We live in a fallen world; sin and temptation are ever-present realities. When we pray to be delivered from evil, we pray that God will rescue us from the consequences of our own sin and the sin that surrounds us. Among contemporary Christians, this can be a neglected prayer. We are accustomed to thinking of ourselves as able to handle life's circumstances, including those less than healthy. This prayer to be delivered from evil is a recognition of the limits of our human goodness and power to resist temptation. In a broken world, we all need deliverance from the forces that warp and distort human flourishing.

The Lord's Prayer can be a model for the prayer life of a new believer. It can be the model for the prayers of any believer, whatever their level of spiritual maturity. Just as it was the prayer that Jesus taught his disciples when they asked to learn how to pray, it can be the prayer we use to teach new believers how to pray.

The Power of Prayerfulness

Prayer is part of God meeting our needs. Through prayer, God protects us where we need protection, changes us where we need change, and allows us to be part of bringing God's kingdom into the world. Prayer protects us from temptations to which we might otherwise succumb. Most importantly, prayer is about building and growing our relationship with God in Christ.

In 2015, I took a sabbatical. Every day that summer, I spent a significant amount of time reading my Bible, reflecting in my journal, and contemplating Scripture and the problems of our family and our congregation. More than once,

I spent an entire morning praying. It was one of the most important things about the time. It had a significant impact on my life and ministry.

Jesus was a person of prayer, and so was the Apostle Paul. Paul knew firsthand the power of prayer. Here is what he wrote to Timothy, his "child in the Lord," near the end of his life:

> I urge, then, first of all, that requests, prayers, intercession and thanksgiving be made for everyone - for kings and all those in authority, that we may live peaceful and quiet lives in all godliness and holiness. This is good, and pleases God our Savior, who wants all men to be saved and to come to a knowledge of the truth. For there is one God and one mediator between God and men, the man Christ Jesus, who gave himself as a ransom for all men - the testimony given in its proper time.
>
> (I Timothy 2:1-6)

For Paul, prayer was the source of spiritual growth, political stability, salvation, and peace. In prayer, the power of God is brought to bear upon the human condition. Paul desired that prayers be made for all people, especially for those in authority, with the goal that Christians and the rest of the world live in peace.

In our prayers, we must recognize, as Paul did, that God does not play favorites. God wants all human beings to be saved and in a deep relationship of love and wisdom with the Eternal. God wants all humans to know Christ and the power of Christ's work on the Cross. The Cross was a testimony, revealing to the world God's message of salvation available for everyone. It was an act of love and solidarity between God and the world (John 3:16-17). The life of prayer is fundamentally a process of being drawn as a disciple into the wisdom and love of God for the benefit of the disciple who prays and for the world Christ loves and desires to be in everlasting fellowship with God. In the last analysis, our prayer life is a part of the process of being filled with the self-giving, transforming wisdom and love of God.

Prayerfulness and the Crisis of Discipleship

At its foundation, the contemporary crisis of discipleship is also a crisis of prayer. The power of God is not unleashed into the world by human strategies, programs, philosophies, or actions. The power of God is released through prayer by the power of the Holy Spirit. The book of Acts records that when the early church prayed, "the place where they were meeting was shaken" (Acts 4:31).

When the Holy Spirit comes, the power of God is present, and the power of God's love shakes our lives, families, churches, and communities. This is not a human shaking. It is a shaking produced by the love and wisdom of God entering into the lives of people and into the organizations and situations in which they find themselves.

The churches of the Northern Hemisphere have relied upon cultural support, financial affluence, advertising, charismatic leadership, and a host of human programs rather than upon the Spirit of God. In the era we are entering, none of those things will enable the church to survive and prosper without prayer and the kind of deep faith that prayer produces. Until then, there will continue to be a crisis of discipleship.

CHAPTER 12

THE WAY OF THE WORD

A Disciple Spends Time in the Word

I spend the first minutes of each day reading the Bible, meditating on the Word, and praying. I have been a Christian since 1977. This practice has been part of my daily routine for most of that time. This has been true as a layperson and a pastor. After all these years, I do not feel right on the days I skip this sacred time, and I believe it makes a difference in who I am and how I behave. (I like to say, "I am not who I should be, but thank God I am not who was was!") This is true of almost every mature Christian I know.

A committed disciple is committed to spending time in Scripture and studying to have the knowledge base required to grow in likeness to and fellowship with the Word Made Flesh. Christians seek to know the truth in every area of life because the truth of God sets us free to be the people God wants us to be. Time in the word of God alone is not enough to be a transformed disciple of Christ, but it is essential to growing in Christ.

To be a disciple of Jesus is to be centered in the witness of Scripture so that we may experience a life-changing relationship with the One of whom Scripture speaks. Much of what we eventually know about God, Christ, the Holy Spirit, and the Christian life is learned by listening to the voice of God in Scripture. However, "knowing about" is useless unless it results in a growing relationship with God in Christ and our likeness to Christ. We have to walk the walk, not just talk the talk. We must be doers, not just hearers of the word (James 2:17).

Importance of Scripture Study

In Acts, Paul leaves Thessalonica for Berea. Earlier, the Thessalonians had resisted the Good News and did not want to hear Paul's message. In Berea, things were different. Luke records: "Now the Bereans were of more noble character than the Thessalonians, for they received the message with great eagerness and examined the Scriptures every day to see if what Paul said was true. Many of the Jews believed, as did also several prominent Greek women and many Greek men" (Acts 17:11-12). Those who earnestly hear the gospel of Christ are the most eager to study their Scriptures. We study Scripture to test the testimony and opinions of others and to grow in our understanding of God, God's world, our fallenness, our constant need for mercy, and our unique place in God's plan to redeem the world.

In perhaps his last letter, Paul underscores the importance of Scripture as he writes Timothy:

> But as for you, continue in what you have learned and have
> become convinced of because you know those from whom you
> learned it. You have known the holy Scriptures from infancy,
> which can make you wise for salvation through faith in Christ Je-
> sus. All Scripture is God-breathed and useful for teaching, rebuk-
> ing, correcting, and training in righteousness, so the man of God
> may be thoroughly equipped for every good work.
>
> (2 Timothy 3:14-17)

Here Scripture is revealed as the source of a deeper understanding of God in Christ, wisdom, the nature of faith, our self-centeredness and sinfulness, and our hope in God through Christ. Scripture was given to us by the Spirit to teach us what God is like, rebuke us of our sins, correct our errors, and train us in the ways of God. Notice that all this implies that Scripture was given to us so we might change, grow, and reach out to a lost and broken world, not just learn information.

The Crisis of Biblical Knowledge

For a long time, pastors, scholars, and students have known that "Biblical literacy" is declining. There was a time when the Bible was found in almost every home in Europe and North America. Reading the Bible in family groups was common before radio, television, and other entertainment media. There was a time when nearly all schools and colleges taught the Bible and literature based upon the Bible. In such a culture, people grew up with some basic understanding of the story the Bible is telling in the culture was formed by the story of the Bible.

This is no longer true. The story of the Bible tells is no longer at the center of our civilization. By the time Dietrich Bonhoeffer wrote *The Cost of Discipleship*, Europe was no longer filled with Christians constantly renewing their life in Christ by internalizing the Word of God. The elites of most European countries and much of America no longer believed in the historic Christian faith. However, these people were still part of a culture where the Christian story formed their fundamental values. Colleges and Universities were still formed by the Biblical story even though many people no longer believed in their Christian heritage and practiced the Christian faith.

Today, in Europe and America, as well as in other parts of the world formed by a post-Christian culture, political, educational, cultural, and artistic leaders are educated into a worldview that excludes the existence of a personal God, the miraculous, private communication with God in prayer, or the presence of a reliable source of the Word. This secular worldview excludes the idea that God gives certain people a word for others, that history is subject to God's sovereign control, and other aspects of the Christian faith. People formed by such a worldview do not intuitively find Christian faith, values, or morals important or realistic.

This situation will not change any time soon. The current crisis of discipleship will continue until disciples of Christ are so profoundly formed by the Christian story that their approach to life and its problems are undeniably different from that of the surrounding culture. The formation and growth of such a people cannot be done by mass media, corporate education, or large, music or entertainment-driven worship services. [1] This kind of formation can only be done by individual Christians and in small communities of people studying the Scriptures, praying, and living out the Christian life together. The situation in our society will not change until there is an entirely different approach to discipleship, one that focuses on living the Bible as much or more than teaching or sharing its truths. New believers must be carefully taught so that they understand the importance of Scripture for their growing faith

A Changed World View and Way of Life

In Romans 12, Paul talks about our need to see the world the way God sees the world when he says:

> I urge you, brothers and sisters, because of God's mercy, to offer your bodies as a living sacrifice, holy and pleasing to God—this is your true and proper worship. Do not conform to the pattern of this world but be transformed by the renewing of your mind. Then you will be able to test and approve what God's will is—his good, pleasing, and perfect will.
>
> (Romans 12:1-2)

Paul, like Jesus, knew that faith should make a difference in behavior. He teaches that if people see the world the way God sees it (with eyes of steadfast, self-giving love) and are transformed in how they view and respond to the world, then Christians will offer God their entire lives and act in ways that please God. For this to happen, Christians must be transformed into bearers of God's love and truth daily.

The Bible is a tool Christians use in their day-to-day life. All tools require skill to use them properly. Generally, the utility of an instrument is only fully available to an artisan trained and experienced in its proper use. Mental tools are no different. The value of the Bible is not in the study of it or even in the memorization of its teachings but in internalizing and consciously and unconsciously learning to live out its truth over an extended time. [2]

As Christians study, memorize, and meditate on the Bible and the story of God and humanity, they learn to "indwell" the Biblical narrative and its principles. Only when the stories and teachings of the Bible are internalized, so they are available as part of our conscious and unconscious perception of the world, do they perform their most important use in guiding thought and action. [3] The goal of Christian Bible study is to, as Paul says in Romans, change the way we see the world so that we see things in light of the wisdom and love of God.

The crisis of faith we face is mainly due to a lack of understanding and internalizing the story of God's love affair with all people of every tribe and nation. The Good News of this love affair is contained in the Bible, particularly in the stories of the life, death, and resurrection of Jesus, of his interaction with people, and of the response of those people to the Good News. Our civilization has lost its unconscious understanding of the nature of God's love and its power to guide us in everyday life and the decisions of everyday life. If we want to be changed by this story and help the world see the difference it makes, we have to take time to be in the word of God and allow it to mold our character and actions.

Transformed by the Word

As Christians study Scripture and meditate upon the One revealed in its pages, we encounter God revealed in the life, death, and resurrection of the Lord Jesus Christ. As Paul says in Romans, "Faith comes from hearing, and the message is revealed through the word of Christ" (Romans 10:17). Later, in Colossians, Paul urges Christians to "Let the word of Christ dwell in you richly as you teach and admonish one another with all wisdom, and as you sing psalms, hymns, and spiritual songs with gratitude in your hearts to God" (Col. 3:16). It is in hearing and internalizing the Word of God so that the word becomes how Christians under-stand the meaning of the world, that they are changed into the image of Christ.

Importance of Meditative Study

In his life and writings, Dietrich Bonhoeffer anticipated the emergence of the worldview that dominates contemporary culture and recommended adopting a daily meditative reading of Scripture, allowing a reader to sense not just the words but a personal communication with God through the words of Scripture. Just a few minutes of meditative reflection on Scripture supports living a life centered on God:

> Meditation is a source of peace, of patience, and of joy; it is like a magnet that draws together all the forces in our life that make for order, it is like deep water that reflects the clouds and the sun on its clear surface. It also serves the Most High by presenting him with a place of discipline, stillness, healing, and contentment in our lives. [4]

Bonhoeffer advised his students (those he was discipling) to choose a shorter text that can be meditated on for an entire week. This is good advice for the new Christian, and one that those of us are inclined to choose too much Scripture or to change scriptures before the first text has been fully internalized. [5] The purpose of meditative study is to allow God to speak in Scripture. This may take days of reading, reflecting, journaling, and prayer. Like any discipline, the discipline of meditation on Scripture does not come easily or quickly. It is important not to become discouraged when a wandering mind or a distracted heart makes it difficult. [6]

Corporate Study of Scripture

It is not enough to study Scripture personally. Christians need one another. Listening to other people in a Bible Study or Sunday School Class enables the Word of Christ to enter and dwell within our hearts through the window of our minds as part of the Christian community. Slowly but surely, we are transformed as we learn to listen as God listens, speak wisely, and love others, even those with whom we disagree. In addition, listening to others, especially wise and experienced teachers, allows one to grow in Biblical knowledge and checks private and erroneous understanding.

There are many ways to grow as a disciple by studying Scripture in groups. There was a time when there was a shortage of good group Bible Study materials.

This is no longer true. There are many excellent Bible Study guides ranging from Sunday School materials, guides to the study of books of the Bible, and topical study guides in areas such as child raising, coming to Christ, doctrine, personal finances, prayer, marriage, theology, etc. All these resources help a group center on Holy Scripture. Not only do resources exist in printed form, but there are many ways to use materials found online or in electronic media. Some of this material is free. [7]

Small Bible groups are not the place for a lecture-oriented study like those seminary students hear or which many Sunday School classes enjoy. The key to a good group Bible study is its character. A study should have three essential characteristics.

1. **Conversation**. People remember about ten percent of what they hear and about eighty percent of what they say. Therefore, lecturing is not the best method for a small Bible Study. The best way for life-transforming Bible study involves personal interaction among people. This means the leader must avoid lecturing too much and not allow anyone else to dominate the discussion.

2. **Open-ended Questions**. It is best to ask questions that enable group members to answer correctly whatever they say. So, questions like, "What did this passage mean to you" are always better than questions like, "What does John Calvin say about this passage?"

3. **Focus on Application**. God is more interested in what Christians put to work in their lives than in how much abstract knowledge they possess. Therefore, it is a good idea to end the study of a passage by discussing the question, "How are we going to live differently now that we have studied this passage?"

God exists in a relationship and wants to draw us into his Triune relationship, Father, Son, and Holy Spirit. Therefore, it is unsurprising that God wants us to hear his Word about His person (Christ) and the Body of Christ as part of a community. God wants Christians, especially new Christians, to listen to this word in private Bible study and corporately in Bible study groups and during worship services.

A commitment to grow as a disciple is essential. God does not want us to be mere hearers of his Word. He wants to transform our lives so we live out that word daily. This is why James says in his letter, "But be doers of the word, and not hearers only, deceiving yourselves" (James 1:22). While it is true that we are saved by grace through faith (Ephesians 2:9), we are also saved for the good works we will do in response to what God has done for us in Christ (2:10). The purpose of our Bible study is not merely to improve our minds and understanding, it is to transform our mind, body, heart, spirit, and soul. This requires more than an objective study.

Listening in Worship

The Bible is read and expounded in worship in nearly every form of Christian fellowship. In many congregations, there is a reading of an Old Testament text, a Psalm, and a lesson from the New Testament. The pastor or other leader will then preach on at least one of these readings. In liturgical congregations, the text is often explained before the reading so listeners can more fully understand the Scriptures of the day. Most pastors spend a significant period preparing to preach carefully, understanding both the text and its application to daily life. Over time, this communal listening within the congregation builds unity, a common understanding, and mutual love and respect.

Basic Group Bible Study

Becoming a mentor for new disciples who want to know more about the Bible is not as complicated as it might seem. Here are just a few helpful rules for developing Bible study skills when ministering to new believers:

- **Use the Bible**. If you are studying the Bible, you need a Bible! If you are in a Bible study group, everyone needs a Bible or a copy of the text the group is studying. In some Bible study materials, the text will be reprinted. In others, people must have a Bible as well as a guide. It is helpful if everyone uses the same Bible version.

- **Prepare in Advance**. Leaders need to prepare in advance. Not only must a leader read the passages, but leaders must also be sure that they understand the passage in a way that can help the group members grow. When ministering to new Christians, one does not need to read multiple commentaries, but it is helpful to research any verse or idea that the leader does not personally understand.

- **Read the Text in the Group**. Much of the Bible began as an orally transmitted message of faith. Therefore, starting by reading the selected passage aloud is always a good idea. This allows a modern hearer to experience something of the oral tradition from which Scripture emerged. Before reading the text, tell the group where the passage can be found.

- **Opening Question.** If you are a group teacher, think out before-hand the first question you will ask. The first question is the most important of all. It opens the discussion and often determines the character of the group's interaction. This question can often take the form of, "What teaching of this verse made an impression on you?" or "What did you find most interesting about this passage?"

- **Reflective Questions**. There is no Bible study unless we engage the text alone or in a group. In reading this passage of Scripture or book, here are some questions you may want to ask yourself about the reader:

  > What immediate message do you hear?

  > What feelings are you having in reading this?

  > What was helpful?

  > How will I act differently because I have read this text?

  > What questions were raised when I read or heard the text?

- **Let Questions Guide the Study.** Ask questions tied to the text and build logically upon one another. If a question is not understood, restate it in different words. Limit initial comments to crucial information for the study. It is essential to focus on the most important aspects of the passage. After the first response to a question, leaders should ask if anyone has a different or additional answer. Don't exhaust a question before moving to the next verse or question. Let the group set the agenda. Above all, realize that most questions do not have a single answer. Affirm those who respond if at all possible.

- **Involve the Imagination.** One crucial technique a teacher or student can use is to involve the whole person: sight, sound, touch, and thought in the study. For example, as the text is read aloud, visualize for yourself or have the group picture the scene. Ask the group to imagine how they would have reacted if they had been present. This is especially useful when studying a story from the Bible or a parable from Jesus.

- **Share Personal Meaning.** Ask yourself, "What does this passage mean to me?" In a group Bible study, the most important thing to know is what the text means to the people present. This does not mean ignoring commentaries or historical understanding. It just means that what changes a person's life is an experience of the power of the Word.

- **Don't Be Afraid.** One barrier to some people exercising gifts for leadership in Bible Study is a fear of not knowing the answer to a question. "I do not know" is always a good answer. If you do not know, offer to study the question and give a solution at the next meeting. Even pastors do not know all there is to know about the Bible. After more than forty years of leading studies, I sometimes don't know the answer to a question. Therefore, no lay leader should be afraid to admit the need to study a question before answering.

- **Stay in One Passage.** One common mistake in small Bible studies is to play "Bible Hopscotch." Most people are unfamiliar with the Bible, and flipping pages makes them nervous. Sometimes, a group must study multiple passages to understand what Scripture means. Much of the time, however, this is not necessary. Staying in a passage allows group members to memorize and remember that passage and will enable that passage to change their lives.

The methods that can be used to study Scripture are numerous. Not every technique that works for one person works for another. People of different generations may prefer other forms of Bible study. For example, I am in my 70s. I do not enjoy media-driven Bible studies as much as younger people in our church. This doesn't mean something is wrong with me or the younger people. It means that different generations, with varying life experiences, prefer different kinds of Bible studies.

Conclusion

Sometime in the Spring of 1977, I attended a little Bible study in Houston, Texas. It was led by a newly graduated seminary student and a few laypeople. We sang a few songs, prayed, studied together, and sang a closing song. This Bible

Study meant enough to me that our family has always been involved in small, intimate Bible Studies. If I look back on my life and ask, "When did I grow the most as a Christian in the least amount of time?" The answer is "In the Friday Night Bible Study."

Interestingly, we called our system of study "Group Grope," meaning that none of us understood the most profound meaning of most of what we studied. We were beginners. Nevertheless, we learned and allowed God's word to change our lives. We grew in Christ. We started businesses and families and shared the struggles of young adulthood. Almost all the Friday Night Bible study members are Christians and Christian leaders in their churches and communities. At least three of us are pastors.

We did not know it but were involved in a transformational Bible study. We were not as interested in becoming Biblical scholars as becoming better Christians. The discipleship crisis in America will not be overcome primarily by scholarly, critical, information-centered studies. It will be overcome by transformational studies led by thousands and hundreds of thousands of ordinary people allowing the Word of God to change them. [8]

More importantly, words alone will not change people in our society. One of the principal elements of postmodernism is a rejection of truth claims. In other words, postmodernism does not necessarily believe that there is anything called "truth" to be found. In such a society, people must see the gospel lived out in an attractive way before they will ever accept the truth and live it out in their own lives. The truth Christians proclaim is not a bid for power over other people. It is an invitation to enter a relationship with the God of infinite love and wisdom who desires to draw the entire human race into one family filled with the joy of the presence of endless love and infinite wisdom. In small discipleship groups, new Christians can experience God's love and wisdom in a life-transforming way.

— CHAPTER 13 —

THE WAY OF SERVICE TO THE WORLD

One cold winter night, I left my office in Bay Village, Ohio to eat pizza with some volunteers. As I walked into Auburn Hall, expecting to see just a few people, I saw over 200 volunteers in yellow T-shirts eating together, having fellowship, and getting last-minute instructions for a ministry called "Respite." Several times a year, Bay Presbyterian Church keeps special needs children so that their parents can have a break from caregiving. When I was there, it took about 200 volunteers to care for about eighty children for a few hours. The night is designed to include fun activities, movies, music, and various experiences for the guests. There is a worship time led by young people at the end of the evening. This ministry has been a part of building the church's reputation as a loving place for children and families.

My former church in Memphis had a retired elder who remains active in local ministry. He was at an age when many people slow down. This particular person, his family, and his small groups within the church did not slow down. Instead, they are active in an inner-city ministry led by a congregation in another denomination. Every week, at least once and sometimes more often, they are at the food pantry, the clothes closet, the Sunday feeding, or another ministry to the poor of Memphis. Much of the time, a few other members attend. Very few, if any, of the persons they serve could make the almost twenty-mile journey to attend our church. Their ministry is an act of love and service to the poor and outcasts. Their Christian action is a witness to Christ to every person who experiences or knows of the ministries..

Post-modern people are often cynical about religion and Christianity in particular. As a result, they are watching to see if Christians live like Jesus and not just talk about him. This means it is just as important to share the Gospel by deed as to communicate by word as we seek to share the wisdom and love of God in Western society. Who we are and what we do is as important as what we say and teach.

Jesus and Love for the Lost

The need for Christians to serve the world should come as no surprise. Jesus did not just preach the good news. Jesus constantly demonstrated the good news by serving others. He healed the physically sick. He cast out demons. He helped people overcome sin and its effects. He confronted injustice. In Jesus, faith and works were perfectly combined in one human life. Christians are not Jesus, but disciples of Christ are empowered to become like Jesus. This means that our faith is not complete without putting it to work in the world, just as did the Messiah.

God cares what Christians do after becoming disciples. He cares so much that he provides each Christian with opportunities to serve the world so that our faith might be seen in our lives. In many passages, Jesus reminds his followers that God expects something from them—to share the self-giving love of God with others, just as Jesus shared that love with the world. In particular, service to the "least of these" is a critical part of the life of a disciple.

Near the end of his gospel, Matthew records the following words:

> When the Son of Man comes in his glory, and all the angels with him, he will sit on his glorious throne. All the nations will be gathered before him, and he will separate the people one from another as a shepherd separates the sheep from the goats. He will put the sheep on his right and the goats on his left.
> Then the King will say to those on his right, "Come, you who are blessed by my Father; take your inheritance, the kingdom prepared for you since the creation of the world. For I was hungry and you gave me something to eat, I was thirsty and you gave me something to drink, I was a stranger and you invited me in, I needed clothes and you clothed me, I was sick and you looked after me, I was in prison and you came to visit me."
> Then the righteous will answer him, "Lord, when did we see you hungry and feed you, or thirsty and give you something to drink? When did we see you a stranger and invite you in, or needing clothes and clothe you? When did we see you sick or in prison and go to visit you?" The King will reply, "Truly I tell you, whatever you did for one of the least of these brothers and sisters of mine, you did for me."
> Then he will say to those on his left, "Depart from me, you who are cursed, into the eternal fire prepared for the devil and his angels. For I was hungry and you gave me nothing to eat, I was thirsty and you gave me nothing to drink, I was a stranger and

you did not invite me in, I needed clothes and you did not clothe me, I was sick and in prison and you did not look after me." They also will answer, "Lord, when did we see you hungry or thirsty or a stranger or needing clothes or sick or in prison, and did not help you?" He will reply, "Truly I tell you, whatever you did not do for one of the least of these, you did not do for me." Then they will go away to eternal punishment, but the righteous to eternal life.

(Matthew 25:31-43)

In the parable, Jesus is teaching both those outside the people of God and those who are part of the people of God.[1] This parable indicates that discipleship under grace involves a call to meet concrete human needs as we are able. We are to see Christ in the poor, the needy, the lost, and the lonely.

Christians are saved for good works "that God has prepared for us beforehand" (Ephesians 2:10). Jesus says that those who love him will do the works he does. John records Jesus as saying, "Truly, truly, I say to you, whoever believes in me will also do the works that I do; and greater works than these will he do, because I am going to the Father (John 14:12). James reminds us that faith without works is a dead thing:

> What good is it, my brothers, if someone says he has faith but does not have works? Can that faith save him? If a brother or sister is poorly clothed and lacking in daily food, and one of you says to them, "Go in peace, be warmed and filled," without giving them the things needed for the body, what good is that? So faith by itself, if it does not have works, is dead

(James 2:14-17).

This chapter focuses on putting our faith into concrete action in our day-to-day lives. This is the key to it all—a lived faith is an alive faith.

The Call to Care

In the last part of Matthew preceding Jesus' arrest, crucifixion, and death, Jesus tells three important stories: the Parable of the Ten Virgins, in which he encourages believers to continue to be filled with the Holy Spirit, the Parable of the Ten Talents, in which he encourages believers to put the gifts, talents and abilities they possess to good use, and the Parable of the Last Judgment in which he enables believers to remember that, when he returns, the human race will be held accountable for their actions in this world, and especially their efforts towards the least, the lost and the outcast.

In the parable, the time between Jesus' ascension and return is now over. God graciously provides time for the human race to care for his creation and grow in likeness to God. Now, that time is complete. It is time for accountability. Jesus is revealed as the Exalted One, before whom every knee rightfully bows and every tongue confesses (Philippians 2:10-11). All the people groups in the world appear for a final judgment (25:2). It is time to review the actual beliefs and behavior of the human race. And so, Jesus separates the peoples of the world who are massed before him as the shepherd separates sheep and the goats (25:32).

When we think of the final judgment, we think of a court of law. During the trial, evidence is presented by both sides. No one is sure exactly what happened, so there is much testimony to establish the facts. The judge and jury must work hard to decide. They must sift through the facts, weigh the evidence, determine who is telling the truth, and the like. At least, that is the way I thought of this parable until I learned about sheep and goats.

In the Holy Land at the time of Jesus, nearly everyone knew what sheep and goats looked like. Sheep were generally white, and goats were black. It was easy to tell them apart. Therefore, the image is not one of a difficult decision by a judge hearing testimony and weighing evidence in a challenging and complicated case. The decision image is of a judge who already knows the facts and can see the decision to be made. God knows our hearts. He knows what we have done and not done during our time on earth. He does not need to ask many questions or review much evidence. He knows.

Jesus tells the sheep, "Come, you whom my Father blesses; take your inheritance, the kingdom prepared for you since the world's creation. For I was hungry, and you gave me something to eat; I was thirsty, and you gave me something to drink; I was a stranger, and you invited me in; I needed clothes, and you clothed me; I was sick, and you looked after me, I was in prison, and you came to visit me" (Matt. 25:34-36). The sheep have done the things that Jesus did while here on earth by loving service to others.

The scene resembles less a judgment in a trial than a reading of a will in a probate court! God says to those who behave as his children, "Come right now and collect your inheritance as Children of God." The sheep, of course, being humble, hardly know what to say because they can't even remember what they've done and are not sure they deserve such an inheritance.

Then, Jesus turned to the goats and said, "Depart from me, you who are cursed, into the eternal fire prepared for the devil and his angels. For I was hungry, and you gave me nothing to eat; I was thirsty, and you gave me nothing to drink; I was a stranger, and you did not invite me in; I needed clothes, and you did not clothe me, I was sick and in prison, and you did not look after me." (Matt. 25:41-43). These people immediately begin to make excuses: They answer, "Lord, when did we see you hungry or thirsty or a stranger or needing clothes or sick or in prison, and did not help you" (v. 41).

Jesus answers these excuses with the words, "I tell you the truth, whatever you did not do for one of the least of these, you did not do for me" (v. 45). Once again, God does not need a lot of testimony because God knows. Jesus says, "Either you believe and live out the Gospel of Love or you don't. Either you believe I am God and try to live as I lived, or you don't. Either you see the world through my eyes, or you don't."

The World is a Place of Great Need

The world is full of obvious needs. Millions of people are starving, without food, water, schools, jobs, shelter, adequate income, and hope. There are many people in prison. Those who travel to poor mission fields see the need in poor nations. However, the need is not just at the end of the earth. Right before our eyes, there is a lot of need. All we must do is read the newspapers, watch TV, look at the Internet, or drive around our city. Everywhere we go, if we open our eyes, we see need. Human need is all around us.

I could pick any city, but Memphis is a good example because we lived in Memphis for a long time. Memphis is one of the poorest cities in America. When we lived there, more than 178,000 Memphians lived in poverty. A good many more lived pretty close to the poverty line. Fifty percent of workers qualified as "low-wage workers." They have family incomes that put them just over the poverty line. These people often have jobs where they do not receive medical insurance and other benefits—any setback results in poverty.

Despite all the efforts of governments and private charities, over the years, Memphis has been getting poorer at a rate of about one percent a year. Poverty in Memphis is not just located in the inner city. It is increasingly found in the suburbs. Memphis has one of the highest crime rates in the United States, and many citizens are imprisoned. There is a lot of substandard housing. In other words, the need is right before the eyes of everyone in Memphis. If you live in a major metropolitan area, your city is not much different.

Wherever We Go, We See

The problem of human needs is everywhere. Wherever we go, we are bound to see it. We can't say to God, "I'm sorry; I never saw the problem." Jesus won't let us off that easy. We can't be like the people in the parable who say, "Lord, when did we see you hungry or thirsty or a stranger or needing clothes or sick or in prison, and did not help you?" (v. 41). The parable said to those in Jesus' day, and speaks to us today, "Don't believe for one moment that God does not know what we've seen and not seen, where we've been and not been, what television news we've watched and not watched, etc." God knows everything and is aware of the depths of our hearts. He knows when we are avoiding doing what we know is right. He will not let us get away with a flimsy excuse: "I just never saw it."

At the beginning of this book, it was discussed that in the West, among those who are relatively affluent, people often feel like they do not need God because they have many material advantages. As we have learned, however, even in the West, there is loneliness, despair, a lack of healthy relationships, and a host of related emotional and spiritual problems. Amid Western affluence, there is great emotional and spiritual poverty and suffering. Physical, emotional, and spiritual needs always confront Christians.

Will We See the World through Jesus' Eyes?

The question Christians face is not "Can we see the world around us through the eyes of Jesus?" but "Will we see the world around us through the eyes of Jesus?" What God calls his people to be and do is primarily determined by where God takes us in life. Wherever God takes us, many physical, emotional, and spiritual human needs exist. Some of those needs involve problems we could, if we would, work on. One of the first things we can do as Christians is develop the eyes of Jesus and become aware of the conditions around us and respond. In the Parable, Jesus assumes that people see needs and alerts us that God is in suffering and love for those in need.

One of the most important churches of the 20th century was a small congregation in Washington, DC, known as the "Church of the Savior." The Church of the Savior never had a large membership. It comprised a series of small missional "congregations," which functioned as churches to a greater or lesser degree. Each group had a mission focus. Over the years, the small groups were instrumental in creating, developing, and sustaining many vital ministries. Its example was so powerful that similar churches and groups were created throughout America. In addition, many other churches have studied the Church of the Savior in designing their ministries and missions.

The Church of the Savior was the brainchild of Gordon and Mary Cosby. Gordon Cosby, the congregation's founder and pastor until his death, was an Army chaplain during the Second World War. By the time he returned home, Cosby had seen how shallow the religious faith of many people could be. He experienced how easy it was for people to behave in non-Christian ways during wartime and began experiments in discipling the soldiers he served during the war. He also believed that the church had failed, not just the men he served during the war but also those who remained back home. He dreamt of forming a different kind of church. The church he dreamed of founding became a reality in the Church of the Savior. [2] Gordon Crosby saw the need and acted.

Soon after its formation, the Church of the Savior determined to conduct its ongoing ministry through small groups. These small groups initially focused on Bible study and learning about Christian faith and practice. Then, Cosby and the Church of the Savior members changed their form and intention. Church of the Savior groups were explicitly designed to conduct missions in and around the Washington, D.C., area. These groups formed the core ministry of the Church of the Savior for most of the last part of the 20th century. Finally, the Church of the Savior itself became a community of churches. When Gordon Cosby died, he was lauded by Christians and on-Christians alike for his work. [3]

Church of the Savior is only one example of what happens when a group of disciples see a need, work together to solve that need, and reach out with the love of Christ to those who need to see and feel the love of Christ. Years ago, I visited Church of the Savior and spent a few days learning about their mission and its impact on Washington, D. C. It was inspirational and informative. Church of the Savior had a highly developed discipleship program embodied in its "School of Christian Living." But, the goal was not to educate disciples but to deploy them as small discipleship groups to meet the needs of their community.

An Action-Oriented Discipleship Strategy

The founders of American pragmatism famously suggested that truth should be judged based on the likely practical impacts when developing an idea or theory. Whatever the academic value of such a theory might be, biblically speaking, there is truth in the notion that truth and action are inseparably intertwined. Jesus is the Way, the Truth, and the Life. It was not what he taught that was the truth; he embodied and remains the Truth. This means that Christ-followers cannot be content with mere head knowledge, nor is it enough for a disciple-maker to instruct a new disciple by teaching abstract principles of Christian discipleship. In the words of the Great Commission, we are not just learning concepts; we are preparing new believers to obey (Matthew 28:20). Obedience is not a concept we know but an action we take.

Whenever one learns a skill, one learns some information. However, one cannot remember a skill without watching someone else and modeling one's actions after theirs. This means that disciple-making programs must be characterized by "learning while doing" and "doing while learning." The question is, "How do we learn while doing?" Here are just a few suggestions:

- From the beginning of a discipling relationship, it is important to remember that discipling relationships, whether personal or in a small discipleship group, do not exist primarily for the benefit and comfort of the Church or its members. The purpose is to reach the world with the love and wisdom of God. Many small groups forget this fact. The Church does not exist for itself but for the world.

- In meeting the needs of people, the gospel itself, God's love for the world, and desire to draw people out of selfish, self-centeredness and into a relationship of loving community with God and others remains central. As a friend reminds me often, "Keep the main thing the main thing." The main thing is faith reaching out in love. This does not mean that we do not meet human needs. We should.

- Take advantage of opportunities that naturally develop to share God's love. In other words, since the need for God's love is all around us, our most effective way of sharing God's love in tangible ways can be that which is closest to us. This requires keeping eyes open where they might be closed.

- Although God does equip the willing and often uses us in surprising ways, a good bit of the time, God uses the talents and the gifts we already possess. When confronted with an opportunity to serve others, a good question is, "Am I or my group equipped to meet this need?"

- The value of planning cannot be overemphasized. Occasionally, faced with an obvious need, people and groups impulsively reach out without planning and end up doing something counter-productive. The best way to avoid failure is to plan.

- Finally, the group leader must be involved in the project to promote discipleship growth. People, like children, do what they see leaders doing, not what leaders tell them they should be doing. Leaders do not have to lead mission projects; it may be counter-productive if they do. However, they do need to be involved.

An Example of a Need Before a Group's Eyes.

As I was writing the above, an example from the past came to mind. Our former church had an extensive foreign mission program. Unfortunately, only relatively few people could be involved. Over time, congregation members felt we should be involved in more local missions. Initially, a small task force considered supporting a public school in a distant neighborhood. The project began well, but over time, the distance and danger of the area became an impediment to success. The church did not have the resources to meet the need.

In addition, our church was in an area of significant economic disparity. There were affluent areas and areas of poverty. One day, members were passing a nearby elementary school. It was in a lovely neighborhood, and the school was brand new. Initially, the group felt it would not be a good idea to adopt the school because they didn't need the church. Then, it discovered that most of the children who attended the school came from poor areas in the district and received various forms of assistance. Many students came from an apartment project near our worship center in which we had attempted an outreach but had been rebuffed by the owner. The group adopted the school to reach children we had already tried to reach.

I was part of a group with the initial project idea. Many of the leaders had been in a discipleship class we had held in the past. Therefore, I volunteered periodically to show support, including when it was difficult to get enough help. Often, I spent the morning of my day off with one or more members of the group and not infrequently with an elder or other leader of the congregation. These were great opportunities to build on already existing discipling relationships. I was not the project's leader, but as pastor, I supported the initiative as needed.

The project was a success. Many members participated. Several small groups undertook small projects to help the school in areas as diverse as reading to children, repairing and building facilities for specific programs, participating in science fairs, assisting with annual testing, and other activities. We had been concerned that there would be resistance to a Christian organization helping a public school. There was absolutely no resistance. They were delighted to have us. In the process, a few people who ordinarily would not have attended our church began participating. Recently, I learned that, although I have been retired for several years, the project continues.

This mission opportunity reveals the importance of keeping our eyes open to the needs around us and being sure we have the right spiritual gifts. We did not have the right spiritual gifts to meet the first need, but we did the second. We were successful because we chose a need we could meet with the resources we possessed. We had bitten off more than we could chew in our first project. In our second project, we met a need we could satisfy. In addition, we had many members with the time, energy, ability, and desire to lead and participate in the second project.

Conclusion

In discipleship, there is an intimate connection between learning and doing. Discipleship is a lifestyle, not a course we take to graduate from church. The wise disciple-maker never forgets the difference between knowing the Bible and being an active disciple. In the late 1970s, I became a Christian. For most of the 1970s nine and 1980s, I was a layperson in Houston, Texas. One early service was to preach at a homeless shelter in the city. In 1991, our family went off to seminary. In seminary, we formed a small ministry for seminary students. After seminary, we went to a poor town in West Tennessee. We were introduced to an impoverished, violent, and drug-infested neighborhood on the first day. Eventually, we helped build a community center in that neighborhood with other churches. Then, we were called to Memphis. Ultimately, our church became involved in an international mission project called "Living Waters for the World." The project began in an exciting way. A small group prayed that God would open the door for us to do a foreign mission in the agricultural area.

One day, a man from another city that I knew called. I did not know this person well, and we had been on different sides of disagreements. He asked if our church would help with a mission project. I didn't want to get involved. I was unnecessarily afraid that becoming involved would harm a project one of my closest friends wanted to begin. I didn't feel like I should say "No," so we invited him to our Session and gave a presentation. To my great surprise, the Session was enthusiastic, and many people became involved almost overnight.

Our church became deeply involved in the ministry. Without being asked, one of our members gave substantial funds to underwrite many expenses. My friend eventually led mission projects in Africa, Mexico, Honduras, and the Philippines. He, his wife, and many other members became national leaders in the ministry and helped train people to install small water treatment facilities. It was a Holy Spirit adventure from beginning to end.

One evening, just before dusk, sitting on the top of a small mountain in the middle of Ghana in West Africa, I stood looking at an installation our congregation had just completed. I was thinking about Jesus' last word, "You will be my witnesses in Jerusalem, and in Judea and Samaria, and to the ends of the earth" (Acts 1:8). Suddenly, as I stood looking at that project in the center of a West African nation, I thought to myself, "Son of Gun, you made it." Chills went through my spine, chills I remember to this very day. God had taken me from Houston to the ends of the earth.

The life of a disciple is to be a life of action. Nothing in this world can be more wonderful and joyful than when we join God's mission to the least and the lost with other disciples of the Risen Lord. He may take us a few blocks away or to the ends of the earth.

CHAPTER 14

LIVING IN TRANSFORMATIONAL COMMUNITY

O f all metaphors, the dearest to many Christians is that of the church as the "Family of God." We all come from human families. Even if our human family is or is not functional, we yearn for a divine family. A primary emphasis of this book is the importance of making and maturing disciples in community. Because new believers are like children in their faith, they need a family just as children need families. [1]

Christian community is intended to be unique. Christians are meant to be part of a loving extended family—the family of God. We are meant to live like a family, in a community with other Christians, sharing our successes, failures, hopes, and our dreams, dashed hopes and dreams, worries, and cares. The church, the community of those who have responded to the call of Jesus to come and follow, is not something optional. It is essential. Becoming a part of a local expression of God's family is fundamental to becoming and being a disciple of Christ.

In an individualistic culture, it is tempting to think of the church as a voluntary society of like-minded people formed to advance a particular set of beliefs. This is not the best way to think of the church. The church is a family where the children are disciples of Christ, growing into a deeper relationship with God. Our families existed before we existed, just as the church existed before we became members—or even believed in Christ. Just as we grow up in a human family, we grow up in the family of God. Just as we received our first teaching in our earthly family, we are intended to receive our first introduction to faith in our Christian family. Just as one day we become leaders in our own family, as we mature, we take on responsibilities in God's family.

Christians will never reach the late-modern or emerging postmodern world with words or ideas alone. [2] In a world that no longer believes in truth, ideas have no power apart from changed lives. In a world that no longer believes in morality, moral theology cannot change people until they have received a new heart from

God. In a world that no longer believes in beauty, words about beauty have no power until people have experienced God's beauty. In a world of isolation and loneliness, people will never be motivated to become part of God's community until and unless they experience the reality of that community in an atmosphere of unconditional love. The church is God's transformational family of love.

Discipling Groups as Families of Christian Growth

Kathy and I have been members of discipleship groups all our married life. We met in a Bible study. We were in Bible studies with other young couples when we were a young couple. We attended a small Sunday School class. We have been a part of small discipling groups with men and women over the years. When I worked as a lawyer, I sometimes had a small group in my law office. When we went to seminary, I met weekly with fellow students, and Kathy grew in fellowship with a group of women. These groups were like family. We kept each other's children, helped in times of stress or pain, and shared our joys, sorrows, shortcomings, and pain.

Since entering full-time ministry, we have been part of discipling groups. For eighteen years, I met with several men weekly. For many years, I taught a yearlong Bible Study for no more than eighteen people. Often, our churches sponsored short-term groups for six or so weeks. Most recently, Kathy and I led "Salt & Light Groups" in our local churches. The size and length of the group are not what matters. The group's love and the teaching and example of its leaders matter most.

Some years ago, we became part of a renewal movement that encourages forming small accountability groups. Over the years, we have been members of several such groups. We've led other discipling groups in our home and at church. We've been members of Sunday School classes. We've attended special groups to learn special skills such as child-raising or managing our money.

Each of these groups changed our lives in meaningful ways. We've grown, helped others, made life-long friends, and experienced the joy of Christ in community with others. Just as Jesus was lifted into heaven and no longer physically with his disciples, most of these groups eventually disbanded as people moved along. Still, each person in each group remains a precious memory. Some of the members of these groups keep in touch after many years apart!

As I initially wrote this, we joined a couple we've known for over thirty years for a social outing. We've never attended the same church. However, they attended a weekly Bible Study in our home for a few weeks when we were young. The friendship created years ago emerges every time we are together. The day before, another couple dropped by our house with their grandchildren. Once again, we met in a discipling group many years ago. Today, we are still Christian friends, helping one another grow and face the new challenges of a new stage of life. The love of discipling groups is a kind that never ends because it was not primarily a human love but a divine encounter.

Personal Relationships Imitating a Personal God

Christians celebrate and worship a God who exists in an intimate, self-giving, life-transforming family relationship. God not only reveals himself to us as Father, Son, and Holy Spirit, God exists as one essence in three distinct persons. These divine persons have an unbroken relationship of eternal, perfect, self-giving love. In other words, God exists as a community (a family) of self-giving mutual love. There is individuality (Father, Son, and Holy Spirit) and relationship (Self-Giving Love) within God's community of love. The Godhead is a divine family.

The divine names: Father, Son, and Holy Spirit, encourage us to see God as a family. This is precisely the relationship Jesus claims and models with his disciples. This has profound implications for the Christian life: If God exists in a family relationship of love, then there is no life as a Christian without being in family-like relationships of love with God and other people. As persons made in the image of God (Genesis 1:26-27), we were made for deep, loving, wise, and powerful life-changing family-like relationships with God, other human beings, and creation. God wants to draw us into the divine life of the Trinity and for us to mirror that divine life in human relationships.

God is love. The love God showed when he "sent his only son" (John 3:16) eternally exists between the Father, the Son, and the Holy Spirit. Only by living as communities of self-giving, unconditional love can the church be the body of Christ as intended. A church that is merely a place for similarly inclined people to meet on Sunday morning, sit in pews, sing, and listen to a talk, is not the church God intended. God meant the church to be a place where people are in a relationship with God and one another. A church is not just a worship service or a hub for Christian education or social action. A church is a group of disciples called to live together and demonstrate God's love to the world. [3]

Jesus says that he desires the disciples to be one just as the Father and he are one (John 17:20-21); he is praying that we might enter the family of God and become life-long participants in the community of God's self-giving love. In other words, Jesus is making us part of God's eternal family. When John calls believers "Children of God" (I John 3:1), he indicates that by faith in Christ and participation in his body, reflecting the wisdom and love of God in our lives and our lives together, we become part of God's family.[4]

People Need Discipleship Groups

It should now be evident that a fundamental principle of disciple-making is that all believers, especially new believers, need to be part of a discipleship group, a small gathering of the family of God seeking to grow in Christ. [5] This was true of the first disciples. It is true of us as well. Just as young children need a healthy family to grow up in, young Christians need a healthy, Christian family. New believers need the experience of growing in Christ in an intimate fellowship of other people trying to grow in Christ.

In the ancient world, a disciple was a learner who followed a teacher and learned from them. The process was twofold:

1. A disciple learned the information that the teacher knew.

2. A disciple came to model the lifestyle of his teacher in a personal, family-like relationship.

For example, Socrates had a group of young men who followed and learned from him. Plato, a disciple of Socrates, taught his disciples, one of whom was Aristotle, who also formed a community of followers. In this way, the teachings of Socrates, Plato, and Aristotle were passed down. We need to recover this ancient way of teaching people and changing lives. Modern universities excel at transmitting information. They are not as good at communicating character. [6]

The internet and "online learning" have made college and other educational opportunities available over the internet. There are even "online seminaries." While these online educational opportunities are suitable for transmitting information and gaining credentials, they cannot, by their nature, provide the discipling Jesus modeled. Jesus personally spent time with his disciples, and they learned as much from what they observed as they were taught. There is an old saying that children "do as they see their parents doing, and not as their parents urge." Disciples model themselves after more experienced disciples, just as children model themselves after their parents for better or worse. [7]

Jesus: Our Model

Jesus may have been single, but he knew how to create a family group. He called ordinary people. He saw their potential. He trained them. He lived with them as if they were his family. He loved them enough to sacrifice his life for them (and us), just as if they (and we) were his biological children. In the end, he called his disciples "Brothers." Then, he set them loose to change the world and build the same community wherever they went. They did precisely that.

How did Jesus form and sustain his earthly family of disciples? Here are a few concrete things he did:

> He called his family of disciples into being (See Mark 1:17).
>
> He shared his life with them (the entire four Gospels).
>
> He prayed for them (John 17:6ff).
>
> He taught them (Mark 1:21).
>
> He loved them (John 13:39).
>
> He rebuked them (Mark 9:36-39).
>
> He allowed them to lead (Mark 6:6-7).
>
> He gave his life for them (Mark 10:45).

A personal, intimate relationship with his disciples was essential to Jesus. From beginning to end, Jesus' conducted his mission in and through relationships with people who were so close to him that they became his family (Matthew 12:50). It is how Jesus fulfilled the most central part of his ministry: getting a small group of men and women ready for the day when they would lead others to faith in God the Father, whom Jesus called "Abba," or "Daddy," by the power of the Holy Spirit. Jesus intended to disciple those he met so that they too would become children of God (John 1:12). As part of this discipleship group, his disciples learned how to be a part of God's family.

It follows that every Christian should have a similar life-transforming experience. Small groups of believers which call people into a relationship with Christ and each other, allow people to share their Christian walk, deepen their prayer life, and experience a life-transforming community are a primary vehicle for the Christian life. These groups are a source of Christian teaching, places of loving care, a source of guidance in difficult times, and provide leadership for a growing fellowship of Christians.

Life after the Resurrection

Life within God's family after his Resurrection and Ascension is not identical with the life of discipleship while Jesus was physically present. When Jesus was physically present, his call was to come and physically follow and be with him (Matthew 4:18-22; Mark 1:16-20; Luke 5:2-11). Those who did not have the faith necessary to leave and follow him did not become disciples. When Jesus ascended into heaven, the apostles' call was to trust and believe in the Risen Christ and, by the power of the Holy Spirit, continue following Jesus, a little and sometimes persecuted fellowship of Christ-followers. He would be invisibly present by the power of the Holy Spirit. After the resurrection, the call was (and is) to follow Jesus, who is present in his people by the power of the Spirit.

In John's Gospel, Jesus promises his disciples that he will not leave them as orphans (a family term). Instead, he will come to them again and again and be with them in a new way (John 14:18). He tells them that it is a good thing that he is going away because when he goes away, the Counselor, the Holy Spirit, will come to them and will both work in the world to bring people to faith and in the lives of his disciples bringing them all the knowledge they will need to have that Jesus could not tell them while physically present on earth (John 16:7-13).

The new way that Jesus is with us is by dwelling within us through faith (Galatians 3:2). This faith is shared, nurtured, grows, and matures inside a Christian family, especially a small community of faith in which we have the freedom to grow and share our successes and failures, strengths and weaknesses, and our gifts where we are not gifted. When Christians develop such communities, we enter into God's life and enable others to experience and enter that life. This is why Jesus could say, "Wherever two or more are gathered in my name, there are I with them" (Matt.18:20).

More than a Program

Hopefully, when people are drawn into God's family of wisdom and love, they find healing, acceptance, and can overcome barriers to Christ-like living. They can see and experience in community the new life Christ promises his believers. There is no other or more effective way to share the gospel. People desire to see the gospel lived out in the lives of people they know and respect. Authentic community is hard to build and maintain in a hyper-individualistic world, where a consumer mentality dominates and people are primarily interested in meeting personal needs. Only with difficulty can Christ-Followers build family-like communities of believers.

Although it is tempting to talk in detail about "small discipling group programs," the point here is that programs come after people. Groups come after community. Community comes after family. Christians must desire to reach out in love before a community can be built by any strategy, however well thought out. Before people can or will respond and reach out with God's love, they must fill their hearts with the love of Christ and the willingness to love others. This transformation occurs at conversion and continues as we experience an ongoing, Christ-centered community.

During my early Christian years, I was blessed to be part of several family-like gatherings of disciples. In some cases, we were all immature Christians. Nevertheless, we gathered weekly. We shared our lives. We shared times of worship, prayer, and Bible study. We read Christian literature and tried to build Christian marriages together. We learned to manage our finances as Christians in small groups. We raised our children together. We tried and failed a lot, but we kept trying. We still are trying together! In the meantime, we built strong relationships that continue to this day. The details of the organization of these groups were never quite the same, but the purpose was the same: to grow in Christ. When people grow in Christ, it is almost inevitable that they will be empowered to share their faith with others somehow.

Because of changes in our society, "worship center churches" that were important in Christianity's history, including recent history, no longer function effectively without a strong discipleship emphasis. Although a few churches will grow due to worship excellence, Sunday school, or other educational programs, the sheer busyness of people today makes this problematic, especially in large metropolitan areas. In addition, most new churches and many churches in Western Europe and parts of the United States do not have the room to create comprehensive Sunday school programs. Therefore, bringing people together in small groups, primarily in homes but in other places, is the best method to disciple them.

If we are to reach out and touch a "Culture of Death," the culture and community dissolving end of the modern world, we need to reach out in love, not just individually but as little communities of believers. Discipleship is not the task of a few highly gifted people. It is the work of all Christians working together. While no strategy is possible without changed lives and Christians who desire to build a life-transforming community, the sheer number of people who need to hear the gospel and have the opportunity to grow in Christ requires some programmatic solution—and small discipleship groups are most likely to succeed.

Family in a Culture that Does Not Value Families

The family of God is vital in a society that does not value family, where many people live and work far from their biological family. [8] The form of life common in America and other cities increases loneliness and isolation among people. Many people live far from their parents and siblings. Because of divorce and other factors, many people do not find a loving community within their biological family. Modern corporate society's structure makes it necessary for some people to move and live away from their families, sometimes across the globe. With the advent of the internet, many people have come to rely upon social media and electronic connections as a substitute for human relationships. Finally, many people are working longer hours than in prior generations. The result is an epidemic of isolation and loneliness.

This loneliness is not healthy. It is pathological. If human beings are meant for community and deep and abiding relationships, then modern life is bound to leave most people disappointed and some deeply wounded. If being fully human requires being in life-giving relationships with God and others, then it is no surprise that our society's deconstruction of the family and stable communities and neighborhoods has devastated people's mental, moral, and spiritual health.

When our society provides community, that community is increasingly political or economic—unfortunately, jobs, corporations, business relationships, and the like offer limited social connection. Businesses do not love anyone as a person, only as an economic unit. Similarly, particularly among the young, belonging to social and political causes may provide some limited sense of connection. However, social causes can only offer a limited amount of love, meaning, and purpose. Our government and political organizations value us as citizens, not as children of God. Exercise classes, hobby groups, and other groups have similar limitations. Human beings were never meant to live as isolated individuals bound together only by work and the laws of society. We were meant for deep, loving, wise relationships.

Unfortunately, at just the moment in human history when the relational, family aspect of the local church is most needed, several factors have limited Christians' ability to respond:

First, over many generations, churches assumed that the loving community of the church would automatically permeate its fellowship. When most people lived in small towns, had relatively strong families, and attended churches where their families had long and strong connections, the church community grew naturally. Pastors and seminaries did not think that they needed to focus on creating life-transforming fellowship. They assumed community would automatically result from the teaching and worship ministries of the local congregation. The massive transfer of population to major cities and the decline of small community churches ended this strategy's effectiveness.

Secondly, major Christian denominations and church groups have adopted a corporate model instead of an organic, family model of church operation and a professional, as opposed to parenting, model of pastoral formation. At the very moment, the size and complexity of our culture were forcing people to live in large cities and anonymous neighborhoods, and the natural ability of people to find spiritual nurture was declining; the church developed in a way that was not easily able to meet the changing reality of people's lives. The corporate model no longer meets the deepest needs of people.

Finally, in the past, many young people were not particularly active in church during their immediate post-high school and college years. When they had children, most returned to their local congregation or a similar congregation where they lived. Unfortunately, young people are delaying families longer and longer. While waiting for family formation, they are constantly bombarded with images of churches as judgmental, corrupt, interested only in money, and backward. Therefore, when confronted by the need for meaning, purpose, and community, they are unlikely to seek the church to answer their deepest needs.

The only way to respond to these challenges is to focus on building a life-transforming community and making and growing disciples. This is not easy. The life-transforming community cannot be accomplished with slick advertising or any other corporate approach to church growth. It requires that people be drawn into a deliberate community that attempts to model God's life among the world's peoples. If we are to respond to the crisis of discipleship in our day, we must learn again what it means to be a part of the family of God—a family called to go and bring others into that family.

CHAPTER 15

DISCIPLESHIP IN AN AGE OF FRAGMENTATION

While held prisoner by the Nazis, Dietrich Bonhoeffer wrote a series of letters published after his death as "*Letters and Papers from Prison.*"[1] In these writings, Bonhoeffer spoke of "Humanity Come of Age" and the need for a "Religionless Christianity." As with all posthumous writings, especially those of someone who died without the opportunity to expound upon ideas formed under the pressure of trying circumstances, Bonhoeffer's concepts of "Humanity Come of Age" and "Religionless Christianity" should be handled carefully. It is not certain precisely what Bonhoeffer meant by the terms, and it is unclear whether he might have abandoned or modified his ideas had he lived. Nevertheless, in our crisis of discipleship, modern Christians struggle with many of the same issues with which Bonhoeffer struggled. His ideas remain relevant to us today.

Humanity Come of Age

The "Humanity Come of Age" of which Bonhoeffer writes is the fruition of the Western Enlightenment and the end of the Modern World, about which we spoke near the beginning of this book. In the Middle Ages, the church was a kind of parent or tutor of European society. The church spoke into people's lives from a position of power and authority. Beginning with the Renaissance and increasing during the Enlightenment and the emergence of the Modern World, humanity entered a period of disengagement from religious authority. Modern science, technology, and contemporary social and economic ideas provided a non-religious foundation for life. So far as Bonhoeffer could see writing from prison in the mid-1940s, the Enlightenment Project had succeeded. [2]

Humanity had indeed come of age, and Christians needed to learn to live and witness in Western society as if there were no God because the societies in which Christians live essentially function as if there were no God. In particular, the church would have to learn to exist without the kind of secular power it wielded in the Middle Ages. This cultural attitude is more pronounced today than when Bonhoeffer wrote.

For a long time, the perceived success of the modern world pushed God out of the consciousness of many people. [3] This feeling was expressed by the mathematician Laplace when speaking of God's relationship with the universe; he said, "I have no need of that hypothesis." Many contemporary people feel no need to seek or have a relationship with God, much less consider God in making day-to-day decisions. They think they have "come of age" and can handle their lives and problems without God. The result for Bonhoeffer was a need for "Religionless Christianity" that can speak into the lives of secular people in words and ways they understand. [4]

Today, thinking people are much less sure about the successes of the modern world. The societies most impacted by the Enlightenment are nearly all experiencing rapid cultural and institutional decay. Western culture is in an accelerating moral, intellectual, aesthetic, political, and cultural decline. Modernity does not have intellectual or practical answers to the decline our culture is experiencing. Remedies that previously seemed likely to succeed, such as social engineering, extensive bureaucracies, technological innovation, corporate power, increased affluence, and the like, increasingly seem part of the problem rather than part of the solution. The violence and alienation of many in Western societies indicate that the Modern World was perhaps not "Humanity Come of Age" but instead, "Humanity in Adolescence." [5]

While no serious thinker recommends a retreat to the premodern world, there is ample evidence that the modern world needs to rediscover and reincorporate the pre-modern world's wisdom into its worldview and cultural reality. Analytical thinking, scientific understanding, technological progress, and material affluence have proven inadequate to meet the human soul's deepest needs, and there is little likelihood that unaided human reason can halt the cultural decline we are experiencing.

In this situation, it is essential to rediscover the values and transcendental concerns that modernity denigrated or ignored. Philosopher of science Michael Polanyi describes the situation in the West as one on which analytical thinking has burned through the intellectual, spiritual, and moral capital of Christian civilization, ending in a kind of intellectual, spiritual, and moral nihilism. [6] The only way out of the situation is to rebuild the intellectual, moral and spiritual foundations of society. In this effort, Christians need to be active participants.

Religionless Christianity

The concept of "Religionless Christianity" is even more challenging to understand than is the notion of "Humanity Come of Age." It is certain that Bonhoeffer did not mean that there was no God, Christ was not the Son of God, the Spirit of God was absent from the world, or the Church had no future. Instead, what Bonhoeffer tried to help others see is that our civilization is in an intellectual and cultural "Dark Night of the Soul," as God purifies the world, Christians, and the church from false notions of God, of discipleship, and the nature and role of the church.

In other words, God is not absent, but cultural realities make it seem as if God is absent. Bonhoeffer puts it this way:

> The God who lets us live in the world without the working hypothesis of God is the God before whom we stand continually. Before God and with God, we live without God. God lets himself be pushed out of the world onto the cross. He is weak and powerless in the world, and that is precisely the way, the only way he is with us and helps us. Christ helps us, not by virtue of his omnipotence, but by virtue of his weakness and suffering. [7]

Bonhoeffer ends by noting that the God of the Bible, who rules the created universe, rules in weakness. In other words, Bonhoeffer continued to believe that there is a God of transcendent wisdom and self-giving love, that Christ is the revelation of that God, and that the Spirit is still at work in the world with the power of cruciform love. However, most people cannot see these realities under modern conditions with its fascination with human intelligence and power. In a world in which power is everything, the wisdom and love revealed on the Cross seems to many to be foolish or a mere illusion.

In such a situation, our role as disciples is to live in the light and presence of God in a world that cannot and will not see that light or experience God's loving presence. Just as, in the early church, the Gospel was seen as "foolishness to the Greeks" (I Corinthians 1:23), the Gospel is also often seen as foolish to modern secular people. In time, the difference faith makes in people's lives will be apparent, and they will rediscover the light of God. In the meantime, Christians will have to witness humility and weakness in an often-hostile world.

Bonhoeffer saw the grim reality that the modern world embraces a worldview and values that exclude God from politics, government, business, social structures, and everyday life. The kind of Christianity, and the kind of church that developed from the time of Constantine through the Reformation to the present decline of the modern world, is inadequate for the new culture of the West, increasingly a world-wide culture that corrodes traditional values and societies wherever it spreads. In response to this reality, God is radically purifying the church to meet contemporary life challenges. The church will not be an honored institution at the core of society, visibly powerful and influential. Instead, others will have to see the influence of the people of God in quiet, sometimes unseen, prayer and action.

Today's world needs a church, purified from its "corporatization," a church that has rediscovered its roots in Christ and deep and abiding relationships of love among members, each serving and sharing the gifts of God with other Christians and the world. A Culture of Death needs to see the victory of life experienced by those who follow the crucified and risen Messiah.

Mission Beyond Self Preservation

In 1944, just before the Normandy invasion, Bonhoeffer wrote an essay to the child of his friends Eberhard and Renate Bethge. In it, he spoke as follows:

> Our church, which has been fighting in these years only for
> self-preservation, as though it were an end to itself, is incapable
> of taking the word of reconciliation and redemption to mankind
> and the world. Our earlier words are bound to lose their force and
> cease, and our being Christians today will be limited to prayer and
> righteous action among men. All Christian thinking, speaking, and
> organizing must be born anew out of this prayer and action. By the
> time you have grown up, the church's form will have significantly
> changed. We are not yet out of the melting pot. Any attempt to
> help the church prematurely to a new expansion of its organiza-
> tion will merely delay its conversion and purification. It is not for
> us to prophesy the day (though the day will come) when men will
> once more be called to utter the word of God that the world will be
> changed and renewed by it. It will be a new language, and it will
> shock some people and yet overcome them by its power; it will be
> the language of a new righteousness and truth, proclaiming God's
> peace with men and the coming of his Kingdom. [8]

These are challenging words. In Bonhoeffer's day, they indicated that the church in Europe was now in disfavor and could do no more than pray and act for the good of the human race. We live in a different time, but Bonhoeffer's words are also vital for us. Too much modern evangelism and discipleship is little more than an attempt to shore up institutions in their current form. While God loves our institutions as we seek to be the family of God in our societies, God is not in the business of shoring them up so that we can avoid necessary change. God wishes Christians to reach out to a lost world with prayer, ideas, solutions, and action to meet the needs of the cultures in which they live.

Bonhoeffer could not see from his prison cell the intellectual, moral, and spiritual crisis into which our culture has increasingly fallen during past decades. The contemporary world's self-assured technological and institutional pride masks its profound inconsistency with human nature and the deepest understanding of science concerning the universe, the human race, and society. Western society, at its moment of Allied victory, was about to enter a period of self-doubt and decline. We live in that decline.

Discipleship beyond Christendom

God is in the business of bringing His Kingdom into the world, not propping up our little kingdoms. Much of modern evangelism and discipleship amounts to shifting church members from one congregation to another, usually larger. God is not interested in our moving existing members from one existing church to another by cleverly devised advertising, programming, and celebrity preaching. God is in the business of expanding his Kingdom of Wisdom and Love in the hearts of all people. God wants to share his wisdom and love with all people so that all people might receive the benefits of the new life Christ offers. God desires his church to be the hands and feet of Christ in accomplishing this mission. The choice for the church is to join God or face irreversible decline.

God remains in control of history and guides the emergence of our new era with his unfathomable wisdom and love. God intends to reach out into the darkness and decay of modern and postmodern society to reach and heal human beings, their families, and ultimately their cultures. As Bonhoeffer realized, we are at a time when the churches of the West are required to concentrate less on institutional survival and more on sharing the Gospel and making disciples in a life-changing, Spirit-empowered encounter with the postmodern world. [9]

Contemporary Christians live at the end of the modern era and the beginning of a new one, an emerging postmodern world. There will be new controversies and adjustments to the Christian faith in a new culture. This does not mean that the Reformation or the modern world's achievements are unimportant or without value, any more than the Reformation meant that the accomplishments of the

Apostolic Age, Age of Church Fathers and Mothers, or Medieval Age were unimportant.[10] The best insights of the Reformation and the modern world must not be lost. One of the modern world's least attractive and most destructive characteristics is its foolish disdain for tradition. If wise, a new era builds upon all that went before it while going beyond past achievements. [11] Christians must model an ability to be faithful to the past and adapt and change to the postmodern age.

It can be hard to accept that we live in a different world, and our churches must adapt to new circumstances. The Roman Catholic and Orthodox churches are thousands of years old. The Reformation era, which was part of the birth of the modern world, has now passed away. We live more than 500 years beyond the days of Luther, Calvin, and the other reformers. The success of Protestant churches was a part of the modern world's success. Nevertheless, it is a stark reality that the Reformation's theological controversies no longer move most people because the circumstances that gave rise to the Reformation no longer obtain. We are in a new world and a new age.

There will probably be changes in Christian theological and liturgical language and forms and a new appropriation of the Biblical text with his revelation of Christ in light of the challenges of a new culture and thought patterns. In particular, we have only begun to understand the dangers and opportunities of a visual and oral, media-based culture. Balancing faithfulness and willingness to adapt is a unique challenge in this area. There will be different forms of "doing church" in this new era, just as the fall of Rome, the Reformation, and the Modern world created new ways of doing church.

When, in *Letters and Papers from Prison*, Bonhoeffer says the West is "not out of the melting pot yet," he means to say that we are not yet out of a time in which it is difficult, if not impossible, to see the contours of the future. I've mentioned that "postmodernism" may not be genuinely postmodern. It may merely be the final, decadent form of modernity. It is too early to tell. The exact contours of the postmodern age and the best and most faithful adaptation of the church are yet to be revealed. Like Bonhoeffer in prison, we cannot see where society is headed. We are not yet out of the melting pot.

The Gospel in the New Era

As Bonhoeffer recognized, Western Christians today live in societies built upon an ideology that excludes the possibility of God from public discourse. [12] Instead of living in denial or attempting to gloss over the situation, Christians are called to share the suffering of God for the world in the world. Showing postmodern people the love of God means living out a life of faith in a world that often considers Christian faith foolish. In many ways, this world is no different than the world that the apostle Paul entered. It is a world inclined to see the cross as foolishness and followers of the crucified God as fools (I Corinthians 1:22-25).

The world can deny or make fun of our theologies and faith but cannot deny the power of wisdom and love in action. For now, Christians will not be honored simply for being Christians. Christian values will not be at the center of public life or decision-making. Going to church on Sunday will not be required for political, social, or economic advancement. It may even be an impediment. For Christians, any advancement will depend on the character and capacity of the individual involved.

Christians are called to minister to society by living and sharing a faith that the world rejects and embodying a lifestyle the world does not respect or admire. Along the way, there will be many failures, martyrs, and false compromises. This is part of living in a melting pot.

In a book entitled *The Great Emergence*, the Christian writer Phyllis Tickle writes about the church in the emerging postmodern society.[13] Tickle observes that Christianity must invent itself about every 500 years at social inflection points, such as the beginning of the Middle Ages and the Reformation. There is truth in this observation. The visible church is a social institution, and like all successful social institutions, it must adapt to a changing culture.

Despite the need for change, the church has always done best when it returned to its roots: faith in Christ, the importance of the Body of Christ, the apostolic tradition, the normative function of Scripture, and holiness and spiritual disciplines. This collection of essays is founded on the belief that whatever shape the future takes will involve individual Christians sharing their faith, making disciples, and living together in a loving community.

Discipleship in this new era will not be without challenges and sacrifices. Life was difficult for the Apostle Paul or Christians in the first centuries after Christ. A Spirit-filled people, "enchanted by the Word of God," will not be easy for the inhabitants of a decaying and often dark civilization to accept or understand. The life of individual Christian disciples will not necessarily be easy.

There will be rejection, persecution, and many who abandon the faith when it does not "work" as they wish it would work. As a pastor, I have watched many people leave the Christian faith when the simple God who answers every prayer and heals every disease is proven to be a false god. The God who always answers our prayers and heals our diseases is an easy God to follow. It is harder to follow a God who dies on the cross and asks that we pick up our crosses and follow him (Matthew 16:24; Mark 8:34; Luke 9:23, 14:27).

Life Among the Fragments

Over and over again, during the last period of his life, Bonhoeffer spoke of living a "fragmentary life." [14] A fragmentary life is a life that cannot achieve the kind of wholeness and integrity for which the human soul yearns because of its circumstances. Bonhoeffer, imprisoned and separated from family, fiancé, and friends, sensed from his prison cell the fragmentariness of his life and the fragmentary life the destruction of German society entailed for his generation. He was, by circumstances, prevented from enjoying anything "normal," life, career, love, family, friendships, and the like. His comrades in the Confessing Church faced a similar inability to enjoy the secure wholeness their parents and grandparents had enjoyed. He and his generation were faced with the reality of incomplete lives. We also confront such a reality.

The conditions of the decline of the modern world and the movement now underway towards a new postmodern reality create difficult circumstances for contemporary Christians. Our culture is gradually decaying into spiritual and moral darkness that involves increasing chaos and violence. Our parents, children, and others we care about and interact with will be profoundly affected by the sickness of our culture. The wholeness we yearn for is beyond us and many of those we love. The result will be a fragmentation of life in which spiritual, moral, and physical wholeness is almost impossible to achieve.

Living faithfully among the fragments of a once-great civilization is uncomfortable, but it is not impossible. Interestingly, Dietrich Bonhoeffer, by all accounts, found wholeness and sainthood in his prison cell. [15] Those with him at the end remarked upon his remarkable peacefulness and cheerfulness. Perhaps the greatest gift Christians can give to a postmodern world is to joyfully and peacefully continue making disciples, praying for people, sharing the gospel, and helping them as they seek a kind of wholeness for their own lives.

At this point, a diversion from Bonhoeffer's analysis is essential. More than prayer and action will be involved in adapting the church to the postmodern world. Just as the initial disciples entered a pagan and hostile Roman Empire, sharing the gospel along the way, contemporary Christians cannot give up sharing the gospel in word and deed. This sharing will involve a few talented apostles like Paul. However, as in the First Century, sharing the gospel will generally involve countless ordinary Christians sharing their faith within the scope of their particular social networks. This will require boldness and courage in our day, just as it did in the First Century. Some will reject, persecute, ignore, and make fun of Christ and Christian testimony. [16]

Implications for 21st-Century Disciples

If we cannot fully see the implications of the emerging postmodern world for the church, we can see enough to know that certain practices are likely to be essential to witness in the new era: [17]

Community

It is virtually certain that the relentless individualism and self-centeredness of the modern era will disappear. There's nothing more likely than that the contemporary notion of the individual as a segregated atom-like monad, seeking its self-development and satisfaction with only limited regard for others, will disappear. Developments in physics, biology, and psychology underscore the absolute importance of relationships in creation, in human life, and in the human soul. The most unambiguous indication of the end of the modern world is the moral and social chaos generated by its unbridled and excessive individualism in families, sexual relationships, business, and politics.

Building small communities of love where people can develop and find wholeness and exercise their spiritual gifts is essential. [18] Just as Jesus created a little redemptive community as he called the first disciples, so disciples in the future will serve society best as they build families and small communities of wisdom and love. Such families and communities will attempt to reflect the character of Jesus in their relationships regardless of the form society takes. In other words, the church will not disappear even if it changes.

More than Words

As Bonhoeffer predicted, prayer and action will characterize Christian families and communities. A world that does not believe in truth will not be a world persuaded by words alone. Only prayer, and visible acts of faith seen in concrete human action, will move the hearts and minds of the emerging generation. [19] It is easy to argue with words. It's hard to argue with the reality of a community of love reaching out to meet the deepest needs of the human heart. It is easy to argue with the abstract idea that "God is love. "It is hard to argue with a person once one sees they act from a center of unselfish, self-giving love. By self-giving love, the world will be saved, not by words. Christians should always have known this, for it was by the love shown on the cross that the savior showed the person and power of God and provided for reconciliation with God in the first place.

Worship and Proclamation

Proclamation of the Gospel will not cease. The Word will be preached and worship conducted in witness to the Risen Christ as it has from the first days of the early church. In this respect, Bonhoeffer may have spoken or implied something beyond what Scripture teaches and history validates. From the beginning of the Christian faith, groups have met to worship, sing, hear the word read and proclaimed, pray, and exalt the living God. This practice will not pass away in the postmodern or any other era. The form of worship and the worshiping community may change, but the reality of the worship of God will not pass away.

The Bible tells the story of the first disciples leaving the Upper Room and going to Jerusalem, Judea, Samaria, and to the ends of the earth armed with the news and proclaiming it even in times of persecution, failure, and economic and personal difficulty. At the center of their proclamation was the Good News that God's promises to Israel were fulfilled in the life, death, and resurrection of Jesus of Nazareth. (Acts 13:16-25). Those who spent time in community with Jesus during his earthly life and witnessed the resurrection were sent into the world to witness what God is doing and has done in Christ. Paul was not one of the original witnesses, nor was Barnabas or others in the second generation of witnesses, but they were also sent. Modern disciples of the Risen Christ are also sent to proclaim the Good News in our day and time, despite scoffers, opposition, and persecution. This is the cost of discipleship.

The Crisis of Discipleship

We are indeed in a time of crisis. The word "crisis" comes from a medieval word that describes a turning point in a disease, a decisive moment from which things will either get better or worse. When I speak of a "crisis of discipleship," the term is used in this sense. We are at a decisive moment at the end of the modern age of Christian witness. A turning point is upon both modern culture and the contemporary church. Things will either continue to get worse or improve—and the decision is ours whether to adapt, serve, and go forward or attempt to maintain existing forms until their inevitable collapse.

This is the crisis of discipleship we face. By the grace of God, we will meet that crisis. The next era of human history will emerge with a vibrant Christian community seeking "the Way, the Truth, and the Life" and serving the world in self-giving love after the example of the One who was and is "the Way, the Truth, and the Life."

ADDENDUM

C risis of Discipleship was written before Kathy and I became acquainted with the work of Peter Scazzero and his wife, Geri, leaders of a ministry known as "Emotionally Healthy Discipleship," the title of his latest book. [1] Recently, I reviewed Greg Ogden's *Transforming Discipleship*. [2] Rewriting *Crisis of Discipleship* to account for the ideas of Scazzero and Ogden would be exceedingly difficult. Yet, their ideas are so important that I added this Epilogue,

Emotional Health and Discipleship

Years ago, Peter and Geri Scazzero reached a crisis in their marriage, ministry, and lives. The Emotionally Healthy Ministry emerged from their commitment to seeking healing and wholeness. In a series of books and programs, the couple examines emotionally healthy spirituality, emotionally healthy relationships, emotionally healthy discipleship, emotionally healthy churches, and emotionally healthy leadership. For women, Geri developed a course known as "The Emotionally Healthy Woman."

One great value of their work is Peter's transparency as he describes his personal journey. Peter came from an Italian immigrant family. His father worked hard, and his mother raised the children. His was not a perfect family. His family life left him with an innate desire to please people and solve problems. Those character traits and intellectual gifts made him ideally suited for ministry. However, there was an element of brokenness as well.

Eventually, Peter became active in campus ministry, went to seminary, and became a missionary in Costa Rica with Geri, now his wife. After a time in mission work, the couple moved to New York City and founded New Life Fellowship Church. It grew and prospered. By 1986, Peter and Geri were experiencing problems that many pastors experience: chronic overwork, emotional exhaustion, family stress, staff and interpersonal issues, betrayals, etc. In the end, after a church split, Peter came to grips with the fact that he was angry, bitter, tired, and depressed. Geri came to grips with the fact that she felt like a single mother because of the programming of her husband's life and no longer felt a call to be a part of Peter's ministry. You must read their books to hear the story in their own words, but it's a wonderful and potentially life-changing read.

Some time ago, one of our children gave me Scazzero's book, *The Emotion-*

ally Healthy Church. [3]   I read it with great interest. Subsequently, [4]   Kathy, my wife, and I purchased and read *Emotionally Healthy Spirituality* and *Emotionally Healthy Relationships* in our small group. Recently, I had an opportunity to put to work the principles of *Emotionally Healthy Discipleship* and *The Emotionally Healthy Leader.* [5]

The basic principle at the base of the Emotionally Healthy series is simple: **Many Christians and their leaders cannot experience the joy of their salvation or attain the level of discipleship they are capable of because of unaddressed emotional problems, usually stemming from their childhood.** Addressing those issues releases emotionally stymied discipleship capacities, promotes healing, and unlocks hidden potential for churches, leaders, and individual Christians. Since churches are made up of humans, creating an emotionally healthy congregation increases congregational effectiveness in making and maturing disciples.

According to Scazzero, there are seven marks of emotionally healthy discipleship:

1.   Becoming emotionally and spiritually formed as a person

2.   Following the Crucified Lord Jesus, not the "Americanized Christ"

3.   Embracing God's gift of personal limits

4.   Discovering the treasures hidden in grief and loss

5.   Making love the measure of maturity

6.   Breaking free of the power of the past

7.   Leading out of weakness and vulnerability

Emotionally Healthy Discipleship can be contrasted with Emotionally Unhealthy Discipleship, which is characterized by the following:

•   Using God to run from God

•   Ignoring the emotions of anger, sadness, and fear

•   Dying to the wrong things

•   Denying the past's impact on the present

•   Dividing our lives into "secular" and "sacred" compartments

- Doing for God instead of being with God

- Spiritualizing away conflict

- Covering over brokenness, weakness, and failure

- Living without limits

- Judging other people's spiritual journey. [6]

Many of us in professional ministry can identify with the list personally and from observing our own, staff, and congregant lives.

Over and over, the command to love God and other people is repeated in the Old and New Testaments. The problem for some people is that they need more emotional maturity and health to obey the command. Addressing emotional blockages to spiritual maturity and discipleship is, therefore, essential. If we are going to love God, and especially if we are going to love other people, we must have the emotional capacity to do so.

Jesus demonstrated both human emotional maturity and spiritual presence as the Light of the World. He accepted the gift of his limits. He was willing to be born in human form, live an ordinary childhood, delay his ministry until the right time, resist temptation, pray, rest when needed, and disappoint followers who expected the wrong things. Ultimately, he was willing to accept the grief and suffering of betrayal, desertion, injustice, violence, and death—a terrible death on a cross. Jesus was emotionally mature.

I cannot speak for all pastors, but I spent much of my professional ministry trying to be successful by the standards of the American Evangelical movement. Church growth, good Biblical programming, meeting endless needs, creating exemplary leadership structure, and a thousand other semi-important things crowded my days and nights with ceaseless activity. In the end, when it was over, like many pastors, I had to ask the tough questions, "Did I do any good?" and "Was it worth it? "Were all the nights spent away from family and friends really necessary?" I had to face critical personal and social failures.

The Emotionally Healthy series of books is not without weaknesses, but the failings are minor compared with the series' strengths. Though using secular psychological models and tools, Scazzero is careful to remain grounded in Scripture and the Christian tradition. One of the series' strengths is the wide range of thinkers quoted and used, especially in the devotional guides, names stretching from the Desert Fathers to contemporary writers like Henri Nouwen. The devotional guides, designed to introduce readers to the notion of the Daily Office, are significant, and many people who take the courses read and use them.

The books and video guides, as are the workbooks, are well-crafted and helpful. I have repeatedly returned to the devotional guides and workbooks to think about certain questions. I recommend *The Emotionally Healthy Discipleship* course for one simple, straightforward reason: I regret that I did not do more to help members, visitors, leaders, and churches in the way Peter and Geri Scazzero recommend. Doing the work the studies require can change your life, improve your walk with Christ, and unlock the hidden potential for joy in Christ.

Transforming Discipleship

As part of revising *Crisis of Discipleship*, I recently read *Transforming Discipleship*. Ogden champions a relational way of making disciples that emphasizes "Triads," groups of three or four individuals, one of whom is a mentor, who embark upon a journey of discipleship together. Because disciple-making is inherently relational, Ogden believes that fundamental transformation best occurs in small, transformational mentoring relationships.

Why should we pay attention to Ogden's ideas? The answer is simple: The evidence supports the conclusion that American churches are doing a poor job of discipleship. As Chuck Colson reportedly said, "American discipleship is 3000 miles wide and an inch deep." Colson voiced this view at a time when the evangelical movement had succeeded in drawing a new generation into its churches. Today, we are experiencing the limitations of focusing on church growth, programs that attract people, and entertainment-centered worship. Nearly all Christian groups, including evangelical congregations, are stable or shrinking.

In *Transforming Discipleship*, Ogden sets out several indicators that American congregations are failing at discipleship:

1. American Churches are not creating proactive disciples who independently reach out to others.

2. American Christians are not taught and do not display a "Way of Life" different from the way of life secular people enjoy.

3. American Christians too easily divide their personal and business lives from their faith, resulting in cultural conformity.

4. American Christians often reflect the values of a materialistic American culture instead of the importance of Christ.

5. American Christianity is excessively individualistic as opposed to communal. [7]

It is hard to argue with these conclusions. American evangelicalism, the branch of Christianity most enthusiastic about the Great Commission, often reduces the Great Commission to "salvation" by "accepting Christ." This divorces evangelism from the Biblical call to "make disciples who obey." A diminished view of salvation and discipleship without support in Scripture has become common. Worse, in many congregations, "joining the church" has become the goal of evangelism, with discipleship relegated to voluntary participation in Sunday School.

Church leaders cannot escape responsibility for the situation. Church leaders like myself, who concentrate on worship, preaching, and maintaining the institutional structure, have not placed disciple-making at the center of their vocation. As Ogden puts it, "Despite Jesus' strategy of calling people from crowds and focusing on a few, we continue to rely upon preaching and programs as a means to make disciples." [8] Many church leaders, and thus many congregations, either have no clear idea of how to create vibrant self-actualizing disciples or deliberately rely on preaching and programming because this is within their comfort zone. We rely upon programs because we do not want to make the personal investment that discipleship requires.

Pastors often become so invested in preparation for worship and being a part of the busyness of the programs and activities of the church that they forget their primary calling to make disciples. Underlying these factors is one fundamental fact: The American church, indeed the churches of Western Culture generally, have failed to make disciple-making central to the mission and ministry of the local congregation and modeled by its leaders. Where the Church operates as intended, there is proactive disciple-making, a distinct difference in the values of Christians and the surrounding society, a unity of church and secular life among believers, a rejection of a materialistic lifestyle, and life-transforming community. These churches are spiritually healthy, whatever their size.

I was involved in larger program-centered congregations for most of my lay and pastoral career. Most such congregations were impacted directly or indirectly by the "Seven Day a Week" model that placed programming at the center of their essentially institutional vision. [10] There are several problems with program-based discipleship:

1. Programs tend to focus on conveying information or knowledge.

As a result, they rarely result in deeper personal relationships with God, other Christians, or a suffering world.

2. Programs focus on a leader preparing to convey the information or knowledge to the participants.

3. Programs focus on structure, regimentation, and standardized results.

4. Programs typically require little accountability from participants who "attend." [11]

For these reasons, programs are unlikely to produce transformed disciples who can share their faith with others and disciple them effectively. I began my ministry in a small congregation, where my motto was "People before Programs." Unfortunately, the pressure of leading larger congregations made me forget the truth in that epigram. In recent years, I have come to believe that my excessive focus on programming was mistaken.

Ogden's solution is to direct churches and their leaders' attention back to the example of Jesus. Although Jesus ministered to "crowds," he invested most of his time and energy into a core group of disciples with whom he shared his life and communicated the life of God. He called the disciples in pairs and one at a time to follow him in the life of discipleship. As time passed, three of the twelve (Peter, James, and John) received special attention and encouragement to grow in their discipleship. Luke indicates that Jesus chose the disciples after a season of prayer. If today's leaders are to follow Jesus, they must pray for a small group of candidates and invest time in them just as Jesus did.

From the beginning, Jesus was preparing his chosen few for the work of the Great Commission. He invested time in teaching and modeling the life of faith for them. He sent them out two by two to practice what they had internalized (Mark 3:14-15). He coached them and supported them in their growth. He refused to do everything and therefore delegated increasing responsibility to them, knowing that the cross lay ahead.

Like Jesus, Paul invested tremendous energy in the few. Silas, Luke, Timothy, Titus, and others mentioned in the New Testament traveled with Paul, shared his life, and received intimate mentorship and teaching in a transparent and supportive relationship. As a result, they were empowered to continue accomplishing the Great Commission. These leaders were formed in the context of a personal relationship.

Ogden is not satisfied with merely reciting the Biblical support for change in how pastors, church leaders, and local congregations create more mature believers. He has specific suggestions as to how this can be accomplished. These suggestions do not take the form of a particular program. To develop the method, one begins with the goal: mature disciples. In Ogden's view, *Mature disciples are formed over time through accountable relationships intended to bring believers to a more profound and life-transforming relationship with Christ.* [12]

To accomplish this goal, Ogden suggests a particular strategy to assist leaders:

1. Life-transforming discipleship is not accomplished by programs but by life investment.

2. Investment in people means having close personal relationships with them.

3. Life investment and deep relationships take time and develop slowly.

4. What Ogden calls "Triads" are an effective means of disciple-making.[13]

Naturally, not every relationship can become a disciple-making relationship. There are conditions for an effective disciple-making relationship:

1. **Trust.** The disciple must trust that the leader is capable of helping develop a deeper relationship with Christ, and the disciple-maker must believe that the disciple has the character, energy, and drive to grow in Christ. Personal accountability, transparency, confession, and active direction must exist for such a relationship. [14]

2. **God's Word.** At the center of any disciple-making relationship is the Word of God. [15]

3. **Mutual Accountability.** There can be no real growth where there is no accountability. In a discipling relationship, this accountability is mutual. [16]

In *Transforming Discipleship*, Ogden sets out a strategy and the details of a particular methodology that is important and much needed. In particular, his focus on intimate relationships of trust and accountability is important.

Conclusion

There are many fine books written each year on the subject of disciple-making. Many of them are written by far more experienced and better disciple-makers than I can claim to be. I hope that *Crisis of Discipleship* has provided a comprehensive look at why an emphasis on discipleship and a return to a more communal approach is needed. I also hope that the personal reflections and experiences I have included are helpful to readers.

Bibliography

Allen, Diogenes. *Christian Belief in a Postmodern World: The Full Wealth of Conviction* (Louisville, KY: Westminster, 1989)

Allen, James. *As a Man Thinketh* (New York: Barnes and Nobel, 1992)

Beare, F.W. "The Mission of the Disciples and the Mission Charge: Matthew 10 and Parallels," Journal of Biblical Literature Vol. 89, No. 1 (March 1970)

Berger, Peter L. *The Sacred Canopy: Elements of a Sociological Theory of Religion* (New York, NY: Anchor, 1967)

----------------. *Rumor of Angels* (New York, NY: Anchor, 1970)

Bishop of Nafpaktos Hierotheos. *Orthodox Psychotherapy: the Science of the Fathers* tr. Esther Williams (Levadia, Greece: Birth of the Theotokos Monastery, 1994)

Bloom, Allan. *The Closing of the American Mind* (New York, NY: Touchstone, 1987)

Bohm, David. *Wholeness and Implicate Order* (London, ENG: Routledge, 1995)

--------------. *On Dialogue* (New York, NY: Routledge, 1996).

Bonhoeffer, Dietrich. *The Cost of Discipleship* Rev. Ed. (New York, NY: Collier Books, 1963)

----------------------. *Life Together* tr. John Doberstein, (New York, NY: Harper One, 1954)

----------------------. *Life Together: The Classic Exploration of Christian Community* (New York, NY: Harper One, 1954)

----------------------. *Letters and Papers from Prison: New Greatly Enlarged Edition* E. Bethge, ed. Second Printing (New York, NY: Macmillan Publishing Company, 1973)

----------------------. *Meditating on the Word* 2nd ed, Translated and edited by David Mcl Gracie (New York, Crowley Publications, 2008).

Breen, Mike & the 3DM Team. *Building a Discipleship Culture: How to Release a Missional Movement by Discipling People like Jesus Did* (Pawleys Island, SC: 3DM Resources, 2011)

Buttrick, George A. *Prayer* (Nashville, TN: Cokesbury/Abingdon Press, 1942)

Calvin, John. *Institutes of the Christian Religion* Vol. 2 John T. McNeill, ed. Ford Lewis Battles, trans. (Philadelphia, PA: Westminster Press, 1960)

De Young, Stephen. *The Religion of Christianity in the First Century* (Chesterton, IN: Ancient Faith Press, 2021)

Downey, Michael. *Altogether Gift: A Trinitarian Spirituality* (Maryknoll, NY: Orbis Books, 2000)

George, Carl F. *Prepare Your Church for the Future* (Tarrytown, NY: Revell, 1991)

Grenz, Stanley J. *A Primer on Postmodernism* (Grand Rapids, MI: Eerdmans, 1996)

Hauerwas, Stanley and Jones, L. Gregory, eds. *Why Narrative? Readings in Narrative Theology* (Grand Rapids, MI: Wm. B. Eerdmans, 1989)

House, Paul. *Bonhoeffer's Seminary Vision: A Case for Costly Discipleship and Life Together* (Wheaton, IL: Crossways, 2015)

Icenogle, Gareth W. *Biblical Foundations for Small Group Ministry: An Integrational Approach* (Downers Grove, Ill: IVP Press, 1994)

Kierkegaard, Soren. *Fear and Trembling* tr, Alastair Hannay, (New York, Penguin Books, 1983)

Kierkegaard, Soren. *Practice in Christianity* Howard V. & Edna H. Fong ed. (Princeton, NJ: Princeton University Press, 1991)

Kittel, G & Friedrich, G, eds. *Theological Dictionary of the New Testament* Abridged ed. (Grand Rapids, Eerdmans, 1985)

Mill, John Stewart. *On Liberty* edited by Currin V. Shields (Indianapolis Indiana: Bobbs-Merrill, Library of the Liberal Arts, 1968)

Loder, James. *The Transforming Moment* 2nd ed. (Colorado Springs, CO: Helmers and Howard, 1989)

Metaxas, Eric. *Bonhoeffer: Pastor, Martyr, Prophet, Spy* (Nashville, TN: Thomas Nelson, 2010)

Mitroff, Ian I. and Warren Bennis. T*he Unreality Industry: The Deliberate Manufacturing of Falsehood and What It Is Doing to Our Lives* (New York, NY: Oxford, 1989)

McIntyre, Alister. *After Virtue* 2nd Ed. (Notre Dame, IN: Notre Dame Press, 1983)

Newbigin, Lesslie. *The Gospel in a Pluralistic Society* (Grand Rapids, MI: Wm. B. Eerdmans, 1989)

------------------. *The Open Secret: An Introduction to the Theology of Mission.* Rev. ed. Grand Rapids, MI: Eerdmans, 1995)

------------------. *Proper Confidence: Faith, Doubt & Certainty in Christian Discipleship.* Grand Rapids, MI: Eerdmans, 1995).

Ogden, Greg. *Transforming Discipleship* (Downers Grove, IL: InterVarsity Press, 2003)

Peterson, Eugene. *Under the Unpredictable Plant* (Grand Rapids, MI: Eerdmans, 1992)

Pierce, C.S. "Questions Concerning Certain Faculties" in *The Essential Charles S. Peirce* Edward C. Moore, ed (New York, NY: Harper & Row)

Polkinghorne, John, ed. *The Trinity and an Entangled World: Relationality in Physical Science and Theology* (Grand Rapids, MI: Wm. B. Eerdmans, 2010)

Polanyi, Michael. *Personal Knowledge: Towards a Post-Critical Philosophy* (Chicago, Ill: University of Chicago Press, 198, 1962), 58-59)

-----------------. *The Tacit Dimension* (Gloucester, MA: Peter Smith, 1983)

-----------------. *Science Faith and Society* (Chicago, IL: University of Chicago Press, 1946)

Rhodes, Michael & Holt, Robby. *Practicing the King's Economy: Honoring Jesus in How We Work, Earn, Spend, Save, and Give* (Grand Rapids, MI: Baker Books, 2018)

Scazzero, Peter. *Emotionally Healthy Discipleship: Moving from Shallow Christianity to Deep Transformation* (Grand Rapids, MI: Zondervan, 2021)

----------------. *The Emotionally Healthy Church* (Grand Rapids, MI: Zondervan, 2003, 2010)

----------------. *Emotionally Healthy Spirituality* updated ed (Grand Rapids, MI: Zondervan, 2017)

----------------. *The Emotionally Healthy Leader: How Transforming your Inner Life will Deeply Transform your Church, Team, and World* (Grand Rapids, MI: Zondervan, 2017)

Schaeffer Francis. *How Should We Then Live: The Rise and Decline of Western Thought and Culture* Rev Ed. (Old Tappen, NJ: Fleming H. Revel, 1976)

Scruggs, G. Christopher. *A Leadership Training Guide for Discipling People: Discipleship Groups at Advent Presbyterian Church* (Unpublished Manuscript, 2000)

----------------------. *Practices and Characteristics for Pastors Renewing Mainline Congregations: Studies from the Presbytery of Memphis* (Unpublished Dissertation, Accepted March 25, 2005)

----------------------. *Path of Life: The Way of Wisdom for Christ Followers* (Eugene, OR: Wipf & Stock, 2014)

----------------------. *Centered Living/Centered Leading: The Way of Light and Love* Rev. Ed. (Cordova, TN: Booksurge Publishing, 2014)

----------------------. *Salt and Light: Everyday Discipleship* (Collierville, TN: Innovo Publishing, 2017)

Smith, Steve & Ying Kai, T4T. *A Discipleship ReRevolution* (Monument, CO: Wigtake Resources, 2011)

Stott, John R. W. *The Message of the Sermon on the Mount* (Downer's Grove, Ill: IVP Press, 1978)

Tickle, Phyllis *The Great Emergence: How Christianity is Changing and Why* (Grand Rapids, MI Baker Books, 2008, 2012)

Trueblood, E. J. *The Dawn of the Postmodern Era* (New York, NY: Philosophical Library, 1954)

Tertullian. *Apology Chapter 39 in Volume 3 The Ante-Nicene Fathers: Translations of the Writings of the Fathers Down to A.D. 325.* Edited by Alexander Roberts and James Donaldson. 10 vols. 1885–1887. (Repr., Peabody, MA, MI: Hendrickson, 1994)

Wink, Walter. *Engaging the Powers: Discernment and Resistance in a World of Domination* (Minneapolis, MN: Fortress Press)

Wright, N. T. *Simply Good News: Why the Gospel is News and What Makes it Good* (New York, NY: Harper One, 2015

Endnotes

Notes to Preface

1. G. Christopher Scruggs with Kathy T. Scruggs, *Salt, and Light: Everyday Discipleship* (Collierville, TN: Innovo Publishing, 2017), hereinafter, "Salt & Light."

2. Dave embodies the relational mode of evangelism and discipleship that this book is intended to illuminate. He began with six persons and built Advent Presbyterian Church in Cordova, TN, into a 1,500-member congregation all through a deep love for people and a willingness to enter into their world in a loving and wise way.

3. Dietrich Bonhoeffer, *The Cost of Discipleship* Rev. Ed. (New York, NY: Collier Books, 1963), hereinafter, "Cost of Discipleship".

Notes to Chapter 1: The Blessed Life

1. A brief survey demonstrates the truth of his proposition. See, for example, Farid Zakaria "Are America's Best Days Behind Us?" *Time Magazine,* Thursday, March 3, 2003 http://content.time.com/time/magazine/article/0,9171,2056723,00.html (Downloaded, June 22, 2019); Eduardo Porter, "America's Best Days May Be Behind It" *New York Times*, January 10, 2016 https://www.nytimes.com/2016/01/20/business/economy/a-somber-view-of-americas-pace-of-progress.html (Downloaded June 22, 2019). Patrice Lewis, "Why Our Best Days Are Behind Us" *WND* https://www.wnd.com/2016/01/why-our-best-days-are-behind-us/ (Downloaded June 22, 2019); Nigel Barber, "Are America's Best Days Over?" *Huffington Post* March 18, 2017 https://www.huffpost.com/entry/are-americas-best-days-ov_b_9487770 (Downloaded June 22, 2019).

2. The point is made powerfully in N. T. Wright's book, *Simply Good News: Why the Gospel Is News and What Makes it Good* (New York, NY: Harper One, 2015), 109ff. In the modern world, we are all subject to a culturally reinforced worldview that considers progress an automatic result of human striving. Recent history casts doubt on this view. What is needed is a new kingdom, not the result of human striving and schemes. Just as the Jews were mistaken to reduce the promise of the Messiah to an earthly kingdom run by a new and improved "Son of David," we are always wrong when we reduce the gospel to a personal, economic, or political agenda. In our culture, Christians need to be prepared to show people the error of expecting God's kingdom to be just like our kingdom only wealthier, politically stronger, and more defensible. When Jesus appeared before Pontius Pilate, and was accused of opposing Caesar, he replied that his kingdom was not of this world (John 18:36). This doesn't mean that we shouldn't be trying to bring his kingdom into this world; it just means there's more to God's kingdom in this world than it will ever know.

3. Matthew 5:1-11.

4. In at least one modern translation of the Beatitudes, the term blessing is translated "Happy." The Old Testament makes clear that, while happiness may result from the blessed life, the blessed life is not constituted by feelings of mere happiness. The blessed life depends on the grace and mercy of God. God is the source of all true blessings. To be blessed is to receive a state of wholeness and holiness and security that only God can provide. It is a gift and act of mercy, not a reward.

5.   Matthew 5:3-12; Luke 6:20-22. The differences between the Matthean and the Lukan descriptions of the Sermon on the Mount are significant, but not for the purposes of this book. In both cases, what Jesus is saying is at odds with what the vast majority of the people in our society see as blessings.

6.   Which is supported by Paul's observation in I Corinthians that the world cannot understand or accept the wisdom of God. It seems foolishness to the human reason without the intervention of God (I Cor. 118-2:16).

7.   The language of Genesis 1 and 9 are nearly identical, indicating God's divine intention remains the same for the fallen human race as it was for the human race at its creation.

8.   Thus, in Proverbs, we read: "Blessed are those who find wisdom, those who gain understanding, for she is more profitable than silver and yields better returns than gold. She is more precious than rubies; nothing you desire can compare with her. Long life is in her right hand; in her left hand are riches and honor. Her ways are pleasant ways, and all her paths are peace. She is a tree of life to those who take hold of her; those who hold her fast will be blessed" (Proverbs 3:13-18).

9.   In Psalms, it also says: "By wisdom, the Lord laid the earth's foundations, by understanding he set the heavens in place; by his knowledge the watery depths were divided, and the clouds let drop the dew (Proverbs 3:19-20).

10.   The term "fear of the LORD" can be difficult for modern readers. When I translate the phrase, I use the word "Deep Respect," which captures the Biblical idea that God is so much greater than human beings that the only proper response before his wisdom and power is a kind of obedient, humble, and absolute respect. See, G. Christopher Scruggs, *Path of Life: The Way of Wisdom for Christ Followers* (Eugene, OR: Wipf & Stock, 2014), at 37, hereinafter, "Path of Life"

11.   It is important not to draw too great a distinction between the wisdom and prophetic writers. Isaiah and Jeremiah, for example, are deeply influenced by and in substantial continuity with the wisdom writers; many of their writings could easily be classified as wisdom writings.

12.   Isaiah speaks of a coming "King of Righteousness," who will usher in a time of blessing for Israel (Isaiah 32:1). In the time of the Messiah, the people will learn to live wisely and receive the blessings of justice and righteousness (v. 2-5). They will finally be led by one under whose leadership they can receive the fullness of blessings for which they longed.

13.   I have written about the awareness of the Old Testament writers that the wise and good life does not guarantee happiness: Job, Ecclesiastes, and some of the Psalms speak of this awareness. Nevertheless, the Old Testament writers believe that God is the source of the blessed life and that it cannot be achieved without following God's laws in faith. See, Path of Life, 165-193.

14.   In my first church, one member of a local congregation criticized me to one of my members for cutting my lawn on Sunday afternoons and coming to the bank in my running shorts. For this person, the "law of Christ," just like the law of the ancient Jews, prohibited any physical work on Sunday and for a religious person to expose himself in any way to others. In other words, this person was a modern Pharisee for all intents and purposes.

15. Francis Schaeffer, *How Should We Then Live: The Rise and Decline of Western Thought and Culture* Rev Ed. (Old Tappen, NJ: Fleming H. Revel, 1976), 205.

16. In Jesus's day, just as in our day, people desired to experience the blessed life. In Jesus's day, just as in our day, people had misconceptions about what it is like to live blessedly. The Jews, like modern Americans, were inclined to suppose that those with sufficient material blessings and economic and political security to relax and enjoy life would experience the blessed life. They, just like many modern Americans, were inclined to believe that if only their own particular political opinion and preferred form of government could be achieved, their lives would be blessed. Jesus came to deconstruct that entire way of thinking.

17. Jesus knew we human beings seldom change our behavior until we experience what life might be like if we adopted another behavior pattern. Therefore, he was not content to talk about the blessed life. Jesus lived the blessed life for all the world to see. He called disciples to live with and observed him. They did not know it at the time, but they were experiencing the blessed life and being trained to share that blessed life with others.

18. One important characteristic of the Gospel of Mark is the way in which it shows Peter and the other disciples as frequently misunderstanding who Jesus was and what He has come to accomplish. They did not understand his Messianic Kingdom, the means by which the Kingdom of God will be established, or the kind of leadership they would be required to exercise in order to accomplish the tasks the Messiah was giving them. It was only in light of the resurrection that they understood the mission of Jesus and the mission he was giving them.

Notes to Chapter 2: Life in the Ruins

1. A good deal of this chapter is based on research done for my Doctor of Ministry Degree. A more heavily footnoted version can be found in G. Christopher Scruggs, *Practices and Characteristics for Pastors Renewing Mainline Congregations: Studies from the Presbytery of Memphis* (Unpublished Dissertation, Accepted March 25, 2005).

2. C. Ellis Nelson, Private conversation (14 March 1994).

3. Diogenes Allen, *Christian Belief in a Postmodern World: The Full Wealth of Conviction* (Louisville, KY: Westminster, 1989), 1.

4. Berger, Peter L. *The Sacred Canopy: Elements of a Sociological Theory of Religion* (New York, NY: Anchor, 1967), 151; see also. Berger, Peter L. Rumor of Angels (New York, NY: Anchor, 1970).

5. One of the most apparent indications that the modern world cannot continue is that this belief in material objects and forces is utterly contrary to our most sophisticated understanding of the universe in which we live. The ultimate nature of material reality seems not to be material. It can be described as disturbances in fields or even as information, but whatever the ultimate reality is, it is not material. Our intellectual leaders, politicians, business people, and religious leaders have hardly begun to accommodate the relativistic, relational, information-centered view of the world favored by contemporary quantum physics and increasingly other disciplines as well.

6. In this way of thinking, God either does not exist or is a part of the only and ultimate reality, the physical universe. Pantheism (the belief that everything is God) is one response

to a materialistic worldview. A more common practical reaction is a movement of religion inward to the human psyche, where it is viewed either negatively as a neurosis or positively as a principle of self-transcendence or wholeness. New age and other similar forms of popular religion emerge from this kind of thinking. In whatever form it takes, the result is a private, inner religion.

7. Right at the beginning, I want to say that this book is not intended to support or condemn any particular denomination or theological perspective. It is the purpose of this book to help and support any and all congregations who wish to reach out in the name of Christ and make disciples regardless of their denomination, theological perspective, or liturgical practices.

8. I have not defined "liberal," conservative," or evangelical, but it does need to be noted that there are differences between the basic belief systems of churches and a chasm between those who attempt to accommodate Christian faith to the modern thought form and those who maintain some form of historic orthodoxy. This book is not intended to present a preference but to hopefully minister to all Christian groups.

9. For a brief, but important outline of the basic elements of this new world-view and its importance for Christian thinking, see Polkinghorne, John. *Quarks, Chaos, and Christianity* Second Ed. (London, England: SPCK Press, 1994, 2005).

10. One of the most precious results of a possible emerging worldview is the recovery of the first proclamation of the Nicene Creed, "We believe in one God, the Father almighty, maker of heaven and earth, and of all things visible and invisible."

11. Allan Bloom, *The Closing of the American Mind* (New York, NY: Touchstone, 1987), Professor Bloom points out what has been my experience both as a student in the late 20th Century and as a teacher. The younger American generations have been indoctrinated into a world view in which "truth" only means valid for me.

12. E. J. Trueblood, *The Dawn of the Postmodern Era* (New York, NY: Philosophical Library, 1954), 19.

13. This essentially utilitarian vision of liberty was given classic exposition by John Stewart Mill in his essay, "On Liberty." While Christians can support much of the utilitarian vision, it is important to remember that we are all essentially connected with others in our society, families, neighborhoods, cities, towns, schools, workplaces, and the like. As a result of this connection, much of our freedom to do as we like must be disciplined by a concern for the lives, views, and interests of others. See, John Stewart Mill, *On Liberty* edited by Currin V. Shields (Indianapolis Indiana: Bobbs-Merrill, Library of the Liberal Arts, 1968).

14. Nowhere is the selfish individualism of contemporary society more evident than in marriage and family life. When the primary goal of human life becomes self-fulfillment, the sacrifice required to maintain strong marriages and families is often absent. In the early 1960s, a convenient fiction was born, holding that even where a marriage had already produced children, divorce was preferable to lovelessness and constant strife. The alternative of learning to love the other unconditionally and creating a home of peacefulness and love was not deemed rational. The result was an epidemic of divorce, weak families, a decline in living standards, and children with profound, unhealed spiritual wounds. Recently, it is increasingly understood that the fiction was just that: a falsehood. Children need both of their parents.

15. "Hedonism" is an ancient Greek moral theory that the ethical life can be reduced to seeking pleasure or happiness and the avoidance of pain or unhappiness. This idea has been important in religious and moral thinkers since Greek times and profoundly impacts some forms of both Pragmatism and Utilitarianism.

16. The pleasure-seeking aspect of modern and emerging postmodern culture is especially evident in the way sexuality both dominates secular politics and the Church's agenda and distorts the Church's life mission. Recent headlines involving the incidence of child molestation by Roman Catholic priests, the continuing divisions in mainline churches over homosexuality, and highly publicized heterosexual clergy misconduct are examples of how the hedonism of modern culture invades the Church. Addiction to pornography, a challenge in many cultures, is made much more pervasive by its easy availability on the Internet. In such a culture, the idea that self-denial and suffering are part of the good life is at odds with the form of life surrounding people.

17. *Christian Belief in a Postmodern World*, previously cited, at 9.

18. Stanley Hauerwas, and L. Gregory Jones, eds. *Why Narrative? Readings in Narrative Theology* (Grand Rapids, MI: Wm. B. Eerdmans, 1989).

19. In ancient Greece, the story of the Iliad with its exaltation of the heroism of Achilles and Hector formed the consciousness of people. Within the great story of the Iliad, kings, warriors, men, women, servants, and the like all found examples of where they could go right in life and how they could go wrong. See Alister McIntyre, *After Virtue* 2nd Ed. (Notre Dame, IN: Notre Dame Press, 1983), Whose analysis I have shortened but largely followed.

20. Robert W. Jenson, "How the World Lost Its Story." First Things Oct. 1993: 19-24.

21. The aspect of postmodernity is especially troubling. Human beings seem to naturally seek to understand their lives as a story, and to place themselves in some way within that story as a character. The loss of narrative inevitably means the loss of place. It also means the loss of identity, meaning and purpose, as it becomes less possible to find a coherent place in the events of daily life.

22. "Consumeritis" is a term I coined for our economy's 'consumer' orientation and how it encourages people to find meaning in acquiring things. The "itis" indicates that Consumeritus is a disease of the soul.

23. Ian I., Mitroff, and Warren Bennis. *The Unreality Industry: The Deliberate Manufacturing of Falsehood and What It Is Doing to Our Lives* (New York, NY: Oxford, 1989), 16.

24. "Timeless," NBC New York (October 3, 2016-December 20, 2018). Timeless is an action drama in the science fiction genre.

25. Walter Wink, *Engaging the Powers: Discernment and Resistance in a World of Domination* (Minneapolis, MN: Fortress Press), 13-31. Wink has written extensively on the powers and principalities and how misunderstanding them can warp Christian thought and action. In my view, Wink is too captive to left-wing ideology, weakening his case. We are all inclined to be controlled by the powers and principalities, not just one group of people.

26. Postmodern thinkers have abandoned hope that any core symbolic world or meta-narrative can provide a unified vision and narrative structure for human life. Unsurprisingly, the result has been cultural decline and growing social chaos. One pressing need in ministering

to postmodern people is to recover the notion of the Bible as a non-violent narrative that provides meaning and purpose as well as the ultimate justification for a free and open society. Stanley J Grenz, *A Primer on Postmodernism* (Grand Rapids, MI: Eerdmans, 1996), 42-43. Interestingly, the Postmodernists propose a metanarrative of their own, denying the possibility of a unified spiritual and moral vision for human life. See also McIntyre, *After Virtue*, previously cited.

27. The term "postmodernity" is used in a variety of ways by various authors. In general, the term "postmodern" is used to describe both a philosophical movement and an emerging cultural reality. The postmodern intellectual period is generally thought to have begun with the philosopher Friedrich Nietzsche and his powerful indictment of both Christianity and Enlightenment optimism concerning human reason. Culturally, the postmodern period is generally thought to have begun to emerge after the First World War, which engendered a tremendous alienation from Western Culture among European intellectual elites. Both the philosophical and cultural aspects of postmodernism are very complex. This study does not presume to provide a comprehensive analysis of postmodern thought. It sought to give a pastoral analysis sufficient for a study of transformational leadership in the contemporary church. Worth noting, however, is that I believe that postmodernism is "here to stay" as a cultural phenomenon, and pastors must minister within postmodern America and to people who are consciously or unconsciously affected by its theory and cultural artifacts. As a cultural reality and as a philosophical movement, postmodernism has aspects that are both positive and negative for the Church and for Christians who witness to Christ under its conditions.

28. See note 4 above.

29. This "religionless paganism" is sometimes referred to as neo-paganism. Just as postmodernity refers to something after modernity, neo-paganism refers to a new form of paganism. The content varies because it is a kind of eclectic collection of beliefs people adopt. What defines them as pagan is the fundamentally manipulative nature of the beliefs, which is to say that the "divine" is put at the heart of human striving. From a Christian standpoint, neo-paganism is both superstitious and idolizing.

30. The emergence of "new age" ideas clearly involves a kind of religion, and even supernatural forces, so the emerging culture is not void of spiritual ideas. When I use the term pagan, I mean a kind of return to the pre-Christian notions of society and morals.

31. Eugene Peterson, *Under the Unpredictable Plant* (Grand Rapids, MI: Eerdmans, 1992), 37.

32. A common experience of pastors and other Christian leaders is the pervasive lack of familiarity with the biblical narrative, even among Christians. The emergence of the Internet, which many people thought would be a great help in alleviating this problem has significantly helped the problem. Unfortunately, there is no substitute for a long-term commitment to study the Bible in some detail. Obviously, some passages are more important than others, and some sections clearer than others. Many of the programs that gave churches and Christian organizations a vehicle for deep discipleship in the past no longer seem to work in the postmodern context.

Notes to Chapter 3: Costly Discipleship

1. Dietrich Bonhoeffer, *The Cost of Discipleship*, previously cited. The book was initially published in 1937. Interestingly, in German, for this book's theme, the title is literally "The

Act of Following." The theme indicates that true Christian discipleship is following Jesus Christ, and the Great Commission of the Church is to create followers of Jesus. After the war, Bonhoeffer's book became famous. Like many influential books, *Cost of Discipleship* is quoted in blogs, sermons, and religious texts (like this one). Unfortunately, it is seldom read outside of college and seminary classes. Part of the problem is that it was originally written in German, a difficult language to translate into English, especially for readers who prefer short sentences and simple language. Another problem is that Bonhoeffer was not a popular writer. He was an academic, and his writing can be difficult to digest. Were it not for his martyrdom under the Nazi Regime, it is doubtful that his books would have been read outside of a narrow academic audience.

2. Id, at 45.

3. Id, at 47.

4. Bonhoeffer was executed on April 9, 1945, by order of Adolph Hitler, one of his last acts before his suicide and death on April 30, 1945. By the time of his death, Bonhoeffer had been imprisoned for just over two years.

5. Western popular Christianity, liberal and conservative, is addicted to just the kind of cheap grace of which Bonhoeffer warned. Modern evangelicalism, in particular, has fallen victim to a popularization of Christian faith that focuses on grace to the detriment of emphasis on the response to grace in faithful living. Cheap Grace is the forerunner of a watered-down form of Christianity in which Christians, like the Corinthians of old, cannot tolerate the meat of the gospel, being addicted to the milk of salvation by grace alone (1 Cor. 3:2). One reason for this book is to encourage local fellowships of Christians in America and the West to begin to seriously build small groups of committed disciplineships within their fellowships.

6. *Cost of Discipleship*, at 47.

7. A recent comment by a well-known mega-Church pastor is but an example. Since the time of the early heretic Marcion (85-160 A.D.), the church has always recognized the continuity and validity of the Old and New Testaments for Christian faith and practice. The difficulties are not new but old as the Christian faith. It is easier to unhitch ourselves from the Old Testament than to learn to understand the way in which Christian faith emerged from First Century Judaism, incorporated the Torah into its emerging Scriptures, and to understand the depth of the inheritance Christianity has from the Jewish Scriptures. This is not said to enter into a debate with this or any other pastor, but to give a concrete example of the temptation to avoid the hard work of discipleship. See, Steve Warren, "Christians need to Unhitch the Old Testament from their Faith: Andy Stanley's Sermon Draws a Backlash" CBS News. Com, May 11, 2018, https://www1.cbn.com/cbnnews/us/2018/may/christians-need-to-unhitch-the-old-testament-from-their-faith-andy-stanleys-sermon-draws-social-media-backlash (Downloaded July 23, 2019).

8. This embodied knowledge of God is what the Orthodox Church refers to as "theosis," or becoming like God. If Christ is the image of God (Colossians 1:5), then in the process of discipleship, disciples become like God by becoming like Christ.

9. Lesslie Newbigin, *The Gospel in a Pluralistic Society* (Grand Rapids, MI: Wm. B. Eerdmans, 1989), 95, 227.

10. It is important for new believers to become part of a group of people seeking to follow Jesus, who

is the Way, the Truth, and the Life. Those who try to follow Christ alone, without belonging to his fellowship, and without accountability for their life of discipleship, inevitably fall short or fail. Those who belong to a fellowship of believers have a better chance of succeeding in the Christian life.

11. See, Michael Green, *Evangelism in the Early Church* rev. Ed. (Grand Rapids, MI: William B. Eerdmans, 1970, 2003).

12. Acts shows the apostles recapitulating in their lives the same mighty deeds, messages of power, and persecution and rejection that Jesus experienced in his life.

Notes to Chapter 4: The Way of a Follower

1. *Cost of Discipleship*, at 70. This is a major focus of Bonhoeffer's work. Bonhoeffer saw that there was a problem in contemporary Christianity which had become so focused on faith and grace it had forgotten the element of obedience and trustful, loving action from a center of faith in Christ.

2. This two-fold act of confessing with lips and believing in the heart is essential to understanding the Christian life. In the Jewish way of thinking, the heart was and is the center of thought and life. While our minds conceive of a thing, it is our hearts that commit us to a course of action. Thus, in proverbs, God as the father figure instructs the believer to put his commandments in his or her heart (See, for example, Proverbs 2:2; 3:3; 7:3).

3. *Cost of Discipleship*, at 70. Bonhoeffer leaves no doubt at this point: "Only the obedient believe."

4. Soren Kierkegaard, *Practice in Christianity* Howard V. & Edna H. Fong ed. (Princeton, NJ: Princeton University Press, 1991), 9-10. It was Kierkegaard's insight that contemporary believers must accept Christ with just the same kind of faith and degree of trust that the first disciples did.

5. *Practice in Christianity*, 233 ff. The quote summarizes what Kierkegaard is after in his entire *Practice of Christianity*. Nevertheless, he distinguishes between imitators who follow and admirers. For one example, "If we have dozed off into this infatuation, wake us up, rescue us from this error of wanting to admire or adoringly admire you instead of wanting to follow you and be like you." Id. Throughout the text, Kierkegaard reminds readers that to believe is to follow and imitate, not to hold a conviction about who Christ was.

6. The Greek word for faith, "pistos," means having faith that results in trust. It has the connotation of obedience. This is why when I translate the term from Greek, I almost always use the term "Trust/Faith." Modern, post-Reformation Christians too quickly fail to grasp that faith trusts and trust. To trust acts in accordance with what is believed. See, Kittel, G & Friedrich, G, eds, *Theological Dictionary of the New Testament* Abridged Ed. (Grand Rapids, Eerdmans, 1985), 849ff.

7. Nothing I say here that involves an interpretation of history should be interpreted as an attack on any Christian group. Orthodox and Roman Catholics, Protestants of all types, and even some of those we refer to as the sects have a perspective on Christian faith. All these perspectives are a mixture of insight and limited human understanding. All are important. My hope is that this study can help all Christian groups in their common goal to reach the world for Christ.

8. Bonhoeffer is emphatic at this point. "If we refuse to take up our cross and submit to suffering and rejection at the hands of men, we forfeit our fellowship with Christ and have ceased to follow him," *Cost of Discipleship*, at 101.

Notes to Chapter 5: The Way of Relationship

1. The Holy Spirit is referred to using many different names in the New Testament, including the Spirit of God, the Spirit of Jesus, the Spirit of Christ, the Holy Spirit, and the Comforter. In all cases, it is a personal name referencing a unique being who is known in a relationship.

2. The doctrine of the Trinity was pounded out and refined at the Councils of Nicea (325) and Constantinople (381). It was pronounced in its current form in the Council of Chalcedon (451). In its current form, it reads: "We believe in one God, the Father Almighty, maker of heaven and earth, of all things visible and invisible. And in one Lord Jesus Christ, the only Son of God, begotten from the Father before all ages, God from God, Light from Light, true God from true God, begotten, not made; of the same essence as the Father. Through him all things were made. For us and for our salvation he came down from heaven; he became incarnate by the Holy Spirit and the virgin Mary, and was made human. He was crucified for us under Pontius Pilate; he suffered and was buried. The third day he rose again, according to the Scriptures. He ascended to heaven and is seated at the right hand of the Father. He will come again with glory to judge the living and the dead. His kingdom will never end. And we believe in the Holy Spirit, the Lord, the giver of life. He proceeds from the Father and the Son, and with the Father *and the Son* is worshiped and glorified. He spoke through the prophets. We believe in one holy catholic and apostolic church. We affirm one baptism for the forgiveness of sins. We look forward to the resurrection of the dead, and to life in the world to come. Amen. The "and the Son" italicized was added in the West and is still a matter of controversy.

3. This is not an essay on apologetics, but it is just at this point that Islam and Christianity diverge. For Islam, God is a monad, a singularity of power to whom believers submit. ("Islam" means submission.) Christianity, on the other hand, sees God as personal, constituted by love, and to be freely accepted, not commanded into submission. If God is an idea, we can understand God, but we can't love God, nor can God love us. The fact that God is love means we can be in a loving relationship with God that takes precedence over and is the foundation of all other actions we take towards God and others.

4. See, David Bohm, *Wholeness and Implicate Order* (London, ENG: Routledge, 1995), 19: "What is implied by this proposal is that what we call space contains an immense background of energy, and that matter as we know it is a small, "quantized" wavelike excitation on top of the background, rather like a ripple on a vast sea."

5. Martin Buber, *I and Thou* 2nd ed. (New York, NY: Scribners, 1958). In his book, he describes the difference between relationships in which we view nature, other human beings, or spiritual realities as persons (a "thou") or objects (an "it"). As a spiritual being, God can be objectified, but not personally known as an object, only as a person.

6. Christians cannot discount the possibility that there are those who, like the Apostle Paul, receive direct communication from God in their calling (Acts 9:1-19; 22:3-22; 26:12-18; Galatians 1:11-24). Ordinarily, there will be no discipleship without a human community of faith. Even Paul had his communities and partners from whom he learned and with whom he grew. Barnabas, who first brought Paul to Antioch, is an example of a mentor in the great apostle's life (Acts 13).

7.   I heard this and read it many years ago. I have looked through my sermons and on the
     internet for the source of his story, but I cannot find it, no matter how hard I look. The idea
     is, of course, that our relationship with God will involve difficulties. In Mother Teresa's
     case, we know that she experienced a long, long period of darkness of the soul when God
     ceased giving her overt indications of his love for her. Mother Teresa continued in the life of
     discipleship for a long time without the consolations of God's unmistakable presence in her
     life

8.   All analogies, including the analogy of marriage, are ultimately incomplete. This is true of
     the analogy of marriage. It is only a useful metaphor to enable human beings to partially
     understand a mystery.

9.   See James Loder, *The Transforming Moment* 2nd ed. (Colorado Springs, CO: Helmers and
     Howard, 1989), 21ff. *The Transforming Moment* is one of the best books on how faith
     initially and subsequently transforms the human person. My analysis of Paul's conversion
     closely follows that of Dr. Loder.

Notes to Chapter 6: Go Share My Life

1.   The Great Commission occurs in some form in each of the Gospels and, again, in Acts. See,
     Matthew 28:18-20; Mark 16:14-20; Luke 24:44-49; John 20:21-23; Acts 1:7-8. In each case,
     there is a sending to witness, and a promise of the presence of the Spirit as the disciples
     undertook to do what they have been asked to do.

2.   The quote is from Rev. Robert Crumpton, who was one of the pastors of Advent
     Presbyterian Church, a former pastor of the Arlington Presbyterian Church, which Advent
     helped to revitalize, and a missionary to Ghana with his wife, Nancy. During my years at
     Advent, Bob was the visitation pastor who shared God's love with every visitor to Advent
     for over fifteen years after his "retirement." The translation is not unique, and I have seen it
     in other places.

3.   I have outlined the importance of wisely living out the teachings of Christ and the Bible in
     much greater detail in *Path of Life: The Way of Wisdom for Christ Followers* (Eugene, OR,
     Wipf & Stock, 2014) and in *Centered Living/Centered Leading: The Way of Light and Love*
     Rev. Ed. (Cordova, TN: Booksurge Publishing, 2014).

4.   See, Steve Smith & Ying Kai, T4T: *A Discipleship ReRevolution* (Monument, CO: Wigtake
     Resources, 2011). This book is the single most important source for learning about T4T,
     which is one of the most important and powerful of disciple-making movements in the
     world today.

5.   This aspect of this story should make us careful about event and media-centered ministries.
     Jesus did not want the disciples to go into a place, preach the gospel, do a few miracles,
     and leave. Instead, he wanted them to stay in one place for a significant amount of time.
     Paul traveled a lot but also spent considerable time in specific cities like Ephesus, which
     indicates that serious disciple-makers should be grounded in a place and a community.

6.   See, Luke 10:17, which applies to yet another sending event. The various gospel narratives indicate that
     his sending before the ultimate sending was a part of Jesus' strategy. See, F.W. Beare, "The Mission of
     the Disciples and the Mission Charge: Matthew 10 and Parallels," Journal of Biblical Literature Vol. 89,
     No. 1 (March 1970), 1-13.

7. *Salt & Light: Everyday Discipleship*, previously cited.

8. See Mike Breen & the 3DM Team, *Building a Discipleship Culture: How to Release a Missional Movement by Discipling People like Jesus Did* (Pawleys Island, SC: 3DM Resources, 2011). Many churches and congregations use this triangle approach.

9. John Polkinghorne, ed., *The Trinity and an Entangled World: Relationality in Physical Science and Theology* (Grand Rapids, MI: Wm. B. Eerdmans, 2010).

10. See *Centered Living/ Centered Leading*, at 165. In *Centered Living, Centered Leading*, I use the term "Deep Love" to describe God's uncreated, self-giving, sacrificial, and steadfast love. The early church adopted the Greek word "Agape" to describe this love.

11. The passages in which one sees that Paul ministered in community are too numerous to mention. The missionary journeys in Acts reflect Paul traveling with others. Often, the final portion of his letters reflect personal greetings to various individual persons important to his ministry. At the very end of his ministry, he asks Timothy to be with him (II Timothy 4:21). There is nothing in the life and ministry of the great missionary apostle to indicate that he ministered other than in community most of the time.

12. As is often the case in interpreting the New Testament, it is essential to recall that the Great Commission is plural. While Jesus speaks to each disciple individually, he also talks to them as a group.

13. See *Cost of Discipleship*, at 256.

14. Dietrich Bonhoeffer, *Letters and Papers from Prison: New Greatly Enlarged Edition* E. Bethge, ed. Second Printing (New York, NY: Macmillan Publishing Company, 1973).

Notes to Chapter 7: Sharing Good News

1. This is why the "Who is on the throne of your life?" presentation of the gospel is often more meaningful to postmodern people. On the other hand, I used the chasm drawing with the young woman in our church I spoke of above, just as I have used other presentations over the years. This is consistent with the notion that we need to adapt our presentation of the Gospel to the needs of those to whom we are trying to communicate.

2. This graphic is found in our book, *Salt and Light, Everyday Discipleship*, previously cited.

3. See Romans 8:1; 1 Cor. 15:22, 2 Cor. 5:17; Eph. 2:9). The spherical use of the phrase indicates that the person who is in Christ is within the sphere of his love and activity. The image is one of location: in Christ.

Notes to Chapter 8: Sharing Your Story

1. There are various theories concerning the writers and compilers of the Gospels. Tradition held that the apostle Matthew wrote Matthew, John Mark, the traveling companion of Peter and Paul, wrote Mark, Luke, the traveling companion of Paul, wrote Luke, and the apostle John wrote John. Critical scholars believe Mark was the first Gospel, with Matthew and Luke each borrowing from Mark. The exact writers are not as important as the observation that the Gospels are primarily edited memories of Jesus.

2. The Greek word "martereo" means "to bear witness." It can also mean to testify. It is also the root from which we get the term "martyrs," i.e., those who die bearing witness to Christ. Gerhard Kittel & Gerhard Friedrich, Eds, *Theological Dictionary of the New Testament* Abridged Ed., Tr. Geoffrey W. Bromily (Grand Rapids, MI: William B. Eerdmans, 1985), 564.

3. Despite its usefulness, this pragmatic definition of truth is limited. Christians do believe that people will be better off if they follow Christ. We don't mean by that that they will always or inevitably be better off. In fact, the benefits of faith can never be fully experienced in this world.

4. As I was completing this book, I was allowed to read Stephen De Young, *The Religion of Christianity in the First Century* (Chesterton, IN: Ancient Faith Press, 2021). De Young very convincingly argues for the continuity between Christianity and Jewish faith in the apostle Paul's life and sees his "conversion" as a "calling." This notion of conversion as calling can be helpful in witnessing to contemporary people, perhaps especially people with a Jewish background.

5. Once again, in my over forty years as a Christian, I have participated in many renewal weekends, meetings, testimony services, and the like. I have heard hundreds of testimonies by ordinary laypersons. Much of the time, there were non-Christians in attendance. Almost without exception, everyone in the room was interested in and moved by the testimony being given. It does not mean that everyone responds to testimony. What is true is that people are rarely offended or dismissive of a testimony.

Notes to Chapter 9: The Way of Dialogue with Others

1. It is a fundamental insight of quantum physics that, at the subatomic level, it is not possible to disengage the observer from the event being examined as was the "Observer-Object" model of investigation dominant in the modern world under the influence of the Newtonian view of science. This insight, first discovered at the subatomic level of physical reality, has implications in other areas and is a part of the emerging postmodern view of science. The American philosopher Charles S. Pearce foresaw this insight in his relational theory of signs. Pearce spoke of the relationship between reality (an object under observation), an interpreter (observer), and the sign used to understand the reality observed. See, C. S. Pierce, "Questions Concerning Certain Faculties" in *The Essential Charles S. Peirce* Edward C. Moore, ed (New York, NY: Harper & Row), 1972.

2. Francis and Edith Schaeffer moved to Switzerland in 1955. Today, there are several L'Abri fellowships all over the world. To learn more, visit www.labri.org. Edith Schaeffer wrote the story of L'Abri in her book by the same name. It is well worth reading. See Edith Schaeffer *L'Abri* (Wheaton, Ill: Crossway Books, 1992).

3. This section is indebted to David Bohm, *On Dialogue* (New York, NY: Routledge, 1996).

4. *On Dialogue*, at 7. My analysis is not intended to eliminate the importance of conversation and debate in developing human knowledge and making decisions. Both have their place. My point is that conversation and debate are not the sole or necessarily the best method.

5. This is an essential difference between what is being said here and what some proponents of dialogue urge. For example, David Bohm believes that dialogue requires suspending our opinions and beliefs. When Bohm urges the suspension of beliefs, he means creating

a situation where we neither believe nor disbelieve. It is doubtful that this is even possible or desirable as to our most deeply held beliefs or the most deeply held beliefs of others. If I believe that God is Love, it is neither necessary nor desirable that I suspend that belief to have a conversation with another person, whether or not they agree or violently disagree with that belief of mine. What is necessary is that I listen with love and be willing to be corrected where I may not be acting or believing consistently with that deeply held belief.

6. Lesslie Newbigin, *Truth to Tell: The Gospel as Public Truth* (Grand Rapids, MI: William B. Eerdmans, 1991), 56. The discussion that follows relies on Newbigin's analysis.

7. Most people resent an exchange in which one person seems to push an agenda or dominate the conversation. This means that we must enter a conversation based on who we are and not armed with a plan to convert others. Although we have conversations that begin and end with a religious premise and are at least partially intended to explain the Christian faith, such discussions almost always start with a question. In short, most conversations that have a gospel component evolve as a part of a larger conversation and relationship among acquaintances.

8. One crucial quality of stories is that a story does not demand or require acceptance or rejection. It simply allows a person to imaginatively enter into a narrative and decide for themself what impact the story has on the hearer. Jesus used parables in just this way. For example, in the story of the prodigal son, while many people see themselves as the prodigal, others see themselves as the older brother or one of the servants.

9. What others communicate to us produces physical responses. Being aware of the physical responses is essential. Experts report that the physical and emotional cues we give another person are as important as our response's actual words. It can take a bit of practice to speak words of love and physically express our concern for the other and resist physical reactions that are inappropriate or unhelpful.

Notes to Chapter 10: Living a Different Way of Life

1. Portions of this chapter are drawn from *Salt & Light*, previously cited, Lesson 10, 99-103.

2. Soren Kierkegaard, *Fear and Trembling* tr, Alastair Hannay, (New York, Penguin Books, 1983), 68.

3. Tradition matters. I have been a pastor for a long time. My churches have all had some form of contemporary worship. While I love modern worship, I sincerely appreciate the liturgical worship of my Catholic and Episcopalian friends. Many weeks, I attend a worship service that connects me to a way of life that is hundreds of years old. Tradition has much to say for itself. The question is, "How should we change to live more like Jesus and the apostles?"

4. Bonhoeffer has an entire chapter of *Cost of Discipleship* devoted to an exposition of Matthew 5:13-16. *Cost of Discipleship*, previously cited Chapter 7, 120-134.

5. In this book, I am taking no position on whether infant or believer baptism correctly understands the sacrament or how the sacraments work. This differs among different groups, and this group of essays is not intended to defend any particular theological position.

6. The purpose of this discussion is to indicate that some form of Baptism is practiced in all Christian fellowships. Most groups that practice infant baptism do not rebaptize

people. Theologically, the person was baptized once, and because God is sovereign and faithful to his promises, there is no need to rebaptize and to do so infers that God was not faithful to the first promise made by the parents. Nevertheless, even in these cases, many congregations perform a renewal of baptism service. In one of my former churches, virtually all the young people renewed their baptismal vows at confirmation.

7.   I am trying in this book to reach out and accommodate all Christian groups, those that are liturgical and those that are not. A close reader will, however, detect that while a Protestant by birth, heritage, and profession, recovery of much that has been lost in the ancient faith is essential, I believe to recovering from the crisis we face in the church.

8.   Cyprian, "One the Unity of the Church" quoted from Timothy Ware, *The Orthodox Church: An Introduction to Eastern Christianity* New Ed. (New York, Penguin Press, 2015), 240.

9.   In this discussion of elementary discipleship, it is not necessary to engage in theological disputes between Protestants, Catholics, and Protestant groups regarding the nature of Christ's presence. Suffice it to say that Christ is present, and the nature of his presence is part of the mystery of the sacrament. As with Baptism, different groups have different ideas about what happens when we celebrate the Lord's Supper. For the purpose of growing as a disciple, it is not so much important which group is correct concerning how the Lord's Supper acts as a means of Grace as that the Lord's Supper changes us. Some congregations celebrate communion weekly. Others celebrate communion monthly, quarterly, annually, or on some other schedule. Disciples make every effort to receive communion whenever it is offered in a way consistent with their particular tradition.

10. Once again, the role and proper method of receiving the sacrament is the subject of differing theological views and denominational practice. This book is intended to help people find a deeper walk, whatever their denominational (or non-denominational) background. For example, some Reformed pastors do not believe in "love feasts" or "renewal of baptism" services. My advice to new Christians is to follow the tradition into which God has called you. My advice to disciple-makers is to follow the guidelines of your particular church related to the sacraments.

11. Dietrich Bonhoeffer, *Life Together: The Classic Exploration of Christian Community* (New York, NY: Harper One, 1954), 110-112.

12. In *Cost of Discipleship*, Bonhoeffer emphasizes that disciples are not called out of the world but into the world. "The disciple must not only think of heaven; they have an earthly task as well" Id, at 130. This earthly task is both our secular occupation and other services to God. There can be no authentic discipleship until and unless the entire being of the disciple and all that the disciple does is for God and the well-being of others.

Notes to Chapter 11: The Way of Prayer

1.   One of the most fascinating attempts to explain away the spiritual dimension of life is found in the occasional articles proclaiming that a group of scientists have found the God part of the human brain and now can explain religious experience. Human beings are complex psychosomatic (mind and body) creatures. Therefore, it is expected that, for human beings to have any awareness of the transcendent, there must be some physical and mental capacity for such awareness. The capacity to be aware of an object, in this case, God, is a requirement for such awareness to develop. See Sharon Begley, "Science Finds God" https://www.washingtonpost.com/wp-srv/newsweek/science_of_god/scienceofgod.

htm?noredirect=on (Downloaded July 15, 2019). The fact that human beings have the capacity for faith in God and prayer to an unseen God is evidence of a reality behind this capacity.

2. The "False Self" is a construction of the human ego designed to project an acceptable persona to others. This constructed False Self divides a person from the True Self, preventing psychological and spiritual wholeness. The human propensity to create a "False Self" is a coping mechanism resulting from our insecurity and inadequacy, usually stemming from childhood, youth, and adolescent anxieties. From a religious perspective, our False Self ultimately derives from alienation from God due to pride and selfishness, unwillingness to accept who God has made us, and failure to recognize God's ultimate trustworthiness to redeem and bless his creatures and creation. Example: I lift myself up because I am prideful but try not to let my pride show. This is a false representation of who I am. I am a prideful sinner and hope not to reveal this truth to others.

3. George A. Buttrick, *Prayer* (Nashville, TN: Cokesbury/Abingdon Press, 1942).

4. Bonhoeffer devotes an entire chapter to the Lord's Prayer in *Cost of Discipleship*. See, *Cost of Discipleship*, 180ff. This follows both Bonhoeffer's discussion and John Calvin's in his Institutes of the Christian Religion. See, John Calvin, *Institutes of the Christian Religion* Vol. 2 John T. McNeill, ed. Ford Lewis Battles, trans. (Philadelphia, PA: Westminster Press, 1960), 3.3.34 ff.

5. See, Matthew 6:9-13; Luke 11:2-4. In this essay, I have used a version found in the confessions and prayer books of certain churches that the older, more traditional language. My churches use a more contemporary version, particularly one in which the word "Trespasses" is translated as "Sin" or "Debts."

6. John R. W. Stott, *The Message of the Sermon on the Mount* (Downer's Grove, Ill: IVP Press, 1978), 146.

Notes to Chapter 12: The Way of Scripture

1. I hesitate to use the phrase "large music or entertainment-driven churches" for fear that the words will be taken pejoratively. Recent years have seen the emergence of large congregations that rely upon sophisticated media and popular music as part of worship. There is nothing wrong with this approach. However, as powerful as the worship experience may be discipleship cannot be done in worship alone, however powerful. Many of these congregations recognize this fact and are deeply committed to developing discipling ministries in their congregation.

2. See, Michael Polanyi, *Personal Knowledge: Towards a Post-Critical Philosophy* (Chicago, Ill: University of Chicago Press, 198, 1962), 58-59.

3. See, Michael Polanyi, *The Tacit Dimension* (Gloucester, MA: Peter Smith, 1983). See also the work of Lesslie Newbigin, *The Gospel in a Pluralistic Society* (Grand Rapids, MI: Wm B. Eerdmans, 1989) for a theological and missional adaptation of Polanyi's notion of indwelling.

4. Dietrich Bonhoeffer, *Meditating on the Word* 2nd. Ed. Tr. David Mcl Gracie (Lanham, MD: Crowley, 1986, 2000), 43.

5.   Id, at 25.

6.   Id, at 26.

7.   When downloading materials from the internet, it is important to remember that not all the materials found on the internet are sound. Many individuals put up materials that do not reflect either the spirit or the words of Christ or the experience of the Church over the centuries. Some of these materials are written by people with little training and limited study.

8.   I make this point with trepidation. It is a fact that transformational Bible studies should form the core of any discipleship program. However, longer and deeper, more theological Bible studies do have a place in the church. In both my congregations, the Disciple Bible Study Series of year-long encounters with the word of God played a big role in the development of leaders and of disciples.

Notes to Chapter 13: The Way of Service to the World

1.   This parable is a part of Matthew's gospel that contains what is often called his eschatological discourses. The section contains a series of stories and parables designed to encourage faithfulness among his disciples, including the lesson of the fig tree (24:32-35) and the description of faithful and unfaithful servants (vv. 36-51),

2.   Elizabeth O'Connor tells the story of the formation of the Church of the Savior in her book *Call to Commitment* (New York, NY: Harper & Row, 1963). My trip to see the Church of the Savior, meet Gordon Cosby, and tour the school of servant leadership that the Church of the Savior created, as well as many of their ongoing ministries, was a highlight of my pastoral life.

3.   This essay is not the place to tell the entire story of the Church of the Savior, which would take a historian with much more talent and time than I possess. For those who wish to know more and study the church and its ministries more deeply, an excellent place to begin is *Call to Commitment*, previously cited. However, *Call to Commitment* is only one of many books and monographs published about the Church of the Savior. There are also many articles and other information about the church, some of which are available on its website.

Notes to Chapter 14: A Disciple Needs a Family

1.   The Bible uses many metaphors for God's community of discipleship. The Church is the "Body of Christ," the "City of God," the "People of God," and the "Family of God." When Jesus came to display the wisdom and love of God in human form, he did not do it alone. He chose a group of followers and poured his life into them. They were his family. During his lifetime, the community grew. When he ascended into heaven, his disciples grew into the church as we know it today. Even now, in some fellowships, fellow believers are called "brother" or "sister."

2.   After lives are changed, and people commit to Christ, the details of our theologies, doctrines, and programs have a role to play in Christian maturity, but usually not before.

3.   Bonhoeffer makes this point both in *Cost of Discipleship,* previously cited, and more directly in his earlier book, *Life Together*. See Dietrich Bonhoeffer, *Life Together* tr. John

Doberstein, (New York, NY: Harper One, 1954). *Cost of Discipleship*, previously cited, Chapter 7, 129-133 and Chapters 29-30, 263-304.

4.   An endearing feature about John and his letters is how he views those he is responsible for discipling as his beloved children. See, 1 John 2:1, 18, 28. In concluding this line of thought, John directly connects the special nature of God's children with a relationship with the Father. "See what great love the Father has lavished on us, that we should be called children of God! And that is what we are!" (I John 3:1).

5.   One difficult matter to decide is the name to call the kind of groups suggested. Many churches have such groups with a variety of names, "Covenant Groups," "Circles of Concern," "Home Churches," "Mission Groups," Life Groups," "Small Groups," and many others. I have called them "discipleship groups" to emphasize their function: to make and develop mature, self-replicating disciples of Christ.

6.   It is important to remember that we are not called merely to transmit information to people. We are called to help people live a new kind of life as a disciple of Jesus. In a sense, every disciple is a child of those who helped that person grow in Christ and is the parent of those whom they are discipling into God-in-Christ's image.

7.   This is not the spot for an extended discussion of seminary education and its challenges. However, it is increasingly important that seminaries not emulate secular academic institutions. Recently, more than one writer has warned that the current and emerging model is inadequate to train religious leaders. See, for example, Paul House, *Bonhoeffer's Seminary Vision: A Case for Costly Discipleship and Life Together* (Wheaton, IL: Crossways, 2015).

8.   Nowhere is the impact of materialism more evident than in arguments over marriage, family life, and human sexuality. Whether the debate is over marital fidelity or alternative forms of sexual expression, the discussion often involves an argument that "people are born this way." At the root of the widespread acceptance of this argument is a materialistic notion of reality in which religious faith may give subjective support to persons but cannot change ultimate reality. On the other hand, among conservative Christians, there is often little difference between how they live and the lifestyle evident in the culture as a whole. In this situation, helping new believers understand the exact nature of the "family of God" and how that family forms and informs our human families is challenging.

Notes to Chapter 15: Living in the Postmodern World

1.   See, *Letters and Papers from Prison*, previously cited.

2.   In a letter dated 16 July 1944, Bonhoeffer traces the emergence of the modern world from the 13th century forward from Herbert of Canterbury through Montaigne, Machiavelli, Descartes, Spinoza, Kant, Fitch, and Hegel as they directed their attention to the autonomy of man and the world. He concludes, "God as a working hypothesis in morals, politics, or science has been surmounted and abolished; and the same thing has happened in philosophy and religion...." Id, at 360.

3.   See *Letters and Papers from Prison*, at 341.

4.   A significant difference between Bonhoeffer's day and our own is that we can see that the Enlightenment project has reached a dead end. It cannot provide an absolute position from

which one can find Truth. It cannot provide a common morality based on reason alone. It cannot provide for the stability of social institutions. It cannot bring peace or social order or agreement upon faith or morals. While its technological achievements are impressive, its moral and spiritual accomplishments are not.

5. In many respects, the modern world was adolescent. The fascination with sex, power, strength, technique, disinterest in inherited wisdom, and the contemporary world's environmental wastefulness all seem immature. In this analysis, what Western society is currently experiencing as "postmodernity" is like "one last drunken hangover of modernity" before growing up.

6. Michael Polanyi, *Science Faith and Society* (Chicago, IL: University of Chicago Press, 1946).

7. *Letters and Papers from Prison* at 361.

8. Id, at 300.

9. I take this as a point of self-criticism: I've spent a lot of my time and energy in institutional maintenance not always related to the expansion of the kingdom of God. The church in the West does need to repent of its focus on institutional expansion and survival. It's quite likely that the postmodern church will look different from the modern churches we have created over the last fifty years. This observation does not mean that our efforts were in vain or meaningless. It means that a new era will require a new and purified church.

10. A genuinely mature postmodern world's characteristics will be the ability to receive, appreciate, and accept the contributions of prior periods of human culture without the arrogant belief that the new and different is better.

11. Just as Luther, Calvin, and other Reformers build upon Augustine and the Church Fathers' work, so also postmodern thinkers will build upon the work of the Reformers and other thinkers of the modern world.

12. See, *The Gospel as Public Truth* previously cited. The work of Newbigin has been my constant companion and inspiration since seminary when I first discovered his work.

13. Phyllis Tickle, *The Great Emergence: How Christianity is Changing and Why* (Grand Rapids, MI Baker Books, 2008, 2012), 22.

14. See, for example, *Life Together*, at 215 and 219.

15. See, Eric Metaxas, *Bonhoeffer, Pastor, Martyr, Prophet, Spy* (Nashville, TN: Thomas Nelson, 2010), 517ff.

16. Perhaps the earliest portrayal of Christ is contained in a piece of Roman graffiti showing Jesus as an ass upon a cross, with the inscription, "Alexamenos worships his god." Pagan Rome made fun of Christians, and the neo-pagan postmodern West will be no different.

17. I have dealt at greater length on the role that small communities will play in meeting the challenges of the emerging postmodern era in the Epilogue to *Path of Life*, previously cited, 221-243.

18. As I was writing this, my dear friend Rev. Dr. David A. Schieber, the founding pastor of

Advent Presbyterian Church in Cordova, Tennessee, USA, sent to me an article from the magazine Presbyterians today about an initiative of the Presbyterian Church (U.S.A.), which is seeking to create 1001 new worshiping communities in the United States of America. They are about half-way to their goal. Most of these communities are small communities of faith ministering to people and areas under serviced by traditional congregations. This effort, whether successful or not, is a sign that the PCUSA sees that the structures and solutions of the 20th Century church are not adequate for the 21st Century. See, M. E. Clary, "1001 New Worshiping Communities: New Life, New Energy, New Expressions of Faith" Presbyterians Today (July-August 2019),40-43.

19. I have experienced this over and over again in the later years of my active, full-time ministry. Young people who grew up in strong local congregations and who are emerging as leaders in the Christian community have a much more wholistic view of faith than their parents and grandparents. People who in past generations might have ended up in the ministry are founding non-profit corporations to solve social problems and share the love of God in practical ways. In prior years, congregations in Memphis sponsored a young man and his family to live in a poor, minority neighborhood and whose life experience is deeply embedded in trying to help one of the poorest neighborhoods in the city. His experience has led him to a ministry of teaching and action to help Christians minister to the poor. See, Michael Rhodes & Robby Holt, *Practicing the King's Economy: Honoring Jesus in How We Work, Earn, Spend, Save, and Give* (Grand Rapids, MI: Baker Books, 2018).

Notes to Addendum

1.   Peter Scazzero, *Emotionally Healthy Discipleship: Moving from Shallow Christian-ity to Deep Transformation* (Grand Rapids, MI: Zondervan, 2021). The Emotional-ly Healthy website is https://www.emotionallyhealthy.org/. The materials necessary to lead folks through emotionally healthy discipleship training are available on their website and most Christian and secular internet book sales sites.

2.   Greg Ogden, *Transforming Discipleship* (Downers Grove, IL: InterVarsity Press, 2003).

3.   Peter Scazzero, *The Emotionally Healthy Church* (Grand Rapids, MI: Zondervan, 2003, 2010).

4.   Peter Scazzero, *Emotionally Healthy Spirituality* updated ed (Grand Rapids, MI: Zondervan, 2017), Today, the Emotionally Healthy Spirituality and Relationship Courses are available as the "Emotionally Healthy Disciples Course," which in-cludes books, study guides, teaching videos, devotional guides, and teaching helps.

5.   Peter Scazzero, *The Emotionally Healthy Leader: How Transforming your Inner Life will Deeply Transform your Church, Team, and World* (Grand Rapids, MI: Zondervan, 2017).

6.   See, *Emotionally Healthy Spirituality*, at 22 and Chuck Olson, *Lead with Your Life* at https://leadwithyourlife.com/book/emotionally-healthy-spirituality/ (Downloaded March 28, 2023).

7.   *Transforming Discipleship*, at 40-46.

8.   Id, at 67.

9.   Id.

10. This phrase is from the important book authored by church consultant Lyle Schaller, *The Seven Day a Week Church* (Nashville, TN: Abingdon Press, 1992). For many pastors in my generation this book and others by Schaller were instrumental in forming our vision of how to grow a vital church.

11. *Transforming Discipleship*, 42-45.

12. Id, at 129. I have rephrased Ogden's exact definition.

13. While I believe that Ogden's idea of discipleship in "Triads" is Biblical and important, my own view is that the number is not as important as that the number of disciples mentored by an individual be small enough that the disciple-maker can invest personally and deeply in each person.

14. Id, at 134-162.

15. Id, 162-168.

16. Id, 168-174.